REVELATION

A Message of Hope for the Christian Church

Stanford E. Murrell

Revelation: A Message of Hope for the Christian Church

Ichthus Publications
P.O. Box 707
Warrendale, Pennsylvania 15095

Our goal is to provide high-quality, thought-provoking books that foster encouragement and spiritual growth. For more information regarding bulk purchases, other IP books, or our publishing services, visit us online or write to support@ichthuspublications.com.

Cover image licensed by Shutterstock.com.

Unless otherwise indicated, all Scripture quotations are taken from the King James Version.

Printed in the United States of America.

ISBN: 978-1-946971-67-8

ICHTHUS

www.ichthuspublications.com

Contents

Foreword

LIKE MANY OTHERS, I have spent a large amount of time trying to understand the book of Revelation from different perspectives. That effort has produced a detailed commentary, *The Royal Reign of Christ*. However, in this work, I have labored to offer a simple yet devotional approach to a book of the Bible that is arguably the most fiercely-debated and misunderstood book in the canon of sacred Scripture. My overarching premise is this: There is no need to read Revelation and unduly speculate on what is being said, nor is there a need to engage in fantastical interpretations. Similarly, there is no need to create a fanciful narrative that keeps changing with the headlines of national and world events. In every time of great tribulation, for the world in general, and the Church in particular, a sure word of prophecy is needed, and given, by the Lord.

Though written in the first century prior to the fall of Jerusalem in A.D. 70,[1] Revelation was written to bless the people of God in every generation, and to comfort individuals. The saints are exhorted to remain patient, and to endure various trials, with the promise of overcoming every Beast, Dragon, and expression of evil. God will not forget those who love and follow

---

[1] For the most comprehensive defense of this dating, see Kenneth L. Gentry Jr., *Before Jerusalem Fell: Dating the Book of Revelation* (Fountain Inn, SC: Victorious Hope, 2010).

the Lamb wherever He goes. The Lamb is going to Calvary. The Lamb is going to the grave. The Lamb is going to heaven. The Lamb is going to come again to establish a new heaven and a new earth wherein righteousness dwells.

If Revelation is read and studied and, after so doing, the heart is left fearful of the future, then the message of the book has been tragically missed. Yet if Revelation is read and there is a sense of confidence, triumph, courage, victory, and hope that no one—and nothing—can destroy, then the narrative has been properly understood. The Lord has given to His people a blessed hope. God has not given His people a spirit of fear, "but of power, and of love, and of a sound mind" (2 Tim. 1:6).

Revelation: A Message of Hope for the Christian Church is to be read and studied afresh for its message from the simple perspective that we are living in a world full of tribulation, yet we need not become disheartened. Christians are given hope for a better tomorrow.

There is a way of understanding the message of Revelation that should satisfy a historical, contemporary, or futurist student of Scripture. When the message of Revelation is fully grasped, the spiritual heart will say, "Even so, come, Lord Jesus" (Rev. 22:20).

Stanford E. Murrell
Viera, Florida

Important Words Associated with Revelation

Apocalyptic Imagery. The book of Revelation follows a literary style known as an "apocalypse." This style of writing uses poetry, allegory, and direct description to form a narrative. Care must be taken to avoid excessive, crass literalism in interpreting the contents of Revelation or the message will be missed. Equal care must be taken in order to avoid a subjective symbolic interpretation. A large part of the narrative is self-interpreting. Because so much of the Bible displays prosaic language, there are, as Dennis Johnson noted, "streams of Old Testament imagery that converge in Revelation." Look for the Old Testament in the New.

Chiasm. What the Spirit has to say to the churches in Revelation 2 and 3 is called, in literature, a chiasm. The word refers to the Greek letter X. It is pronounced, ky'-az-um, and can be defined, technically, as an intersection or crossing of two tracts. In literature, a chiasm is a writing style that uses a unique repetition pattern for clarification and emphasis. Time and again, the church will be told to hear what the Spirit has to say. Look for various literary repetitions in Revelation.

Date of Revelation. Students of the Bible examine external and internal evidence to date a particular book. External evidence is the witness of persons, and/or events, outside the Scripture. Internal evidence is the witness of the document itself. The late date for Revelation is considered to be between A.D. 90 and A.D. 95. The early date for Revelation is considered to be sometime before the fall of Jerusalem in A.D. 70. In this work, the early date is assumed, though not defended, in order to avoid any distraction from the main message God has for His people in every generation throughout the history of the Church.

Interpretive Symbolism. At least twenty-six times in Revelation, a symbol is explained or interpreted by the author. Look for key words and phrases of explanation such as: "are," "which are," "is," "which is," etc.

Jezebel was the daughter of Eth-a-baal, king of Tyre and Sidon. She became the wife of Ahab, the eighth king of Israel. Ahab reigned for twenty-two years in Samaria, 875 B.C. – 853 B.C. While Ahab may have been the king, his wife Jezebel was a dominating personality, and compelled him to establish the worship of the idols of Phoenicia, especially the storm god Baal-Melcarth. A temple and alter were built in Samaria, and a lovely grove was set aside for orgies to the goddess Asherah.

> And in the thirty and eighth year of Asa king of Judah began Ahab the son of Omri to reign over Israel: and Ahab the son of Omri reigned over Israel in Samaria twenty and two years. And Ahab the son of Omri did evil in the sight of the Lord above all that were before

> him. And it came to pass, as if it had been a light thing for him to walk in the sins of Jeroboam the son of Nebat, that he took to wife Jezebel the daughter of Ethbaal king of the Zidonians, and went and served Baal, and worshipped him. And he reared up an altar for Baal in the house of Baal, which he had built in Samaria. And Ahab made a grove; and Ahab did more to provoke the Lord God of Israel to anger than all the kings of Israel that were before him (1 Kgs. 16:29–33).

Literal. There is a school of interpretation that insists the narrative in Revelation be interpreted in a literal way. When the Bible speaks of Satan being bound for a thousand years, the understanding would be a period of one thousand literal years (even though the Greek term chilioi; is plural of uncertain affinity). When the Bible speaks of an angel having a key to the bottomless pit, where Satan will dwell for a thousand years, that is to be understood as a literal angel, having a literal key, to a literal pit without a bottom. While there is much to be said for a literal interpretation of the Bible, allowance must be made for symbols, figures of speech, types, and apocalyptic writing. One helpful way to understand Revelation is to read the book *aloud* in order to enter into the spirit of the narrative. There is a blessing that comes to those who *hear* the Revelation read, for the mind has a chance to grasp the pictorial images being conveyed, while the heart is nourished on the spiritual substance of the images.

Millennialism. The idea of the "millennial" or "thousand-year period" of the reign of Christ and the binding of Satan is only found in Revelation 20 and much attention has been paid to that word. Different theologies have emerged.

There is *premillennialism*, which teaches Christ shall return prior to the millennial.

There is *postmillennialism*, which advocates the return of Christ after the millennial.

There is the *amillennialism*, position which teaches a present millennial, whereby the rule and reign of Christ is a current reality and shall be until His Second Advent, and then throughout the new heavens and new earth.

The presuppositional thought guiding this work, is that the message of Revelation transcends all theological biases to unite the hearts of God people in the faith that the Church shall overcome, and be triumphant, and the Devil shall be defeated, because our God reigns.

Because this position is taken, because the message of Revelation is universal, and applicable to every generation, time has not been taken trying to identify specific cities, or personages, other than what the Scripture identifies itself in context.

Nicolaitans. The Nicolaitans were a religious sect, or party, which arose during the apostolic church period to challenge the truth taught by Christ. The Lord declared that He hated the doctrine of the Nicolaitans, and so must the saints.

False doctrine is to be hated by the Saints. "But this thou hast, that thou hatest the deeds of the Nicolaitans, which I also hate" (Rev. 2:6).

False doctrine is hated by the Savior. "So hast thou also them that hold the doctrine of the Nicolaitans, which thing I hate" (Rev. 2:15).

False doctrine finds converts, even within the professing church of Christ. "So hast thou also them that hold the doctrine of the Nicolaitans, which thing I hate" (Rev. 2:15).

While the church of Smyrna hated false doctrine, the church of Pergamos embraced false doctrine. According to tradition, the Nicolaitans believed that it was lawful to eat food offered to idols. They mixed idolatrous worship with the worship of Christ. The Nicolaitans also denied that God was the creator of the world. They promoted the community of women whose conduct was in the highest degree licentious. "For it seemed good to the Holy Ghost, and to us, to lay upon you no greater burden than these necessary things; That ye abstain from meats offered to idols, and from blood, and from things strangled, and from fornication: from which if ye keep yourselves, ye shall do well. Fare ye well" (Acts 15:28, 29).

While there is no positive evidence, several early church fathers contended that Nicolas, one of the first seven deacons chosen by the apostles in Acts 6:5, was the founder of the Nicolaitans. If Nicolas was one of the original seven deacons, then his life serves as a warning that it is not how well one begins in the Christian faith that matters, but, rather how well one ends.

Oratorio. An oratorio is a musical composition that includes orchestra, choir, and soloists.

Revelation Chapter 1

Introduction to the Revelation

1 The Revelation of Jesus Christ, which God gave unto him, to show unto his servants things which must shortly come to pass; and he sent and signified *it* by his angel unto his servant John:

The word "revelation" (Gk. *apokalupsis*) means, "to reveal." It is a word of disclosure. It is where we get the term, *apocalypse*. The Revelation is an unveiling, or the lifting of a veil so that something can be understood. The truth the Church is given is something that can be understood, for it is about Jesus Christ, and comes to us in this manner. God speaks to Jesus, Jesus speaks to the angel, the angel speaks to John, and John speaks to the Church. When we hear the Word of God, we hear it through ministers.

John ministered to the Church by writing the words of the vision given to him by the angel. The angel is a ministering spirit to those who are the heirs of salvation. The angel himself was ministered to by the Eternal Word, Jesus Christ, who in turn was ministered to by the Father. When we realize that the Revelation comes to us in a marvelous way, the value of the message is enhanced, and so is the one of whom the message speaks—Jesus Christ. Then, because we have been ministered to, because we have been blessed, we are to go forth and share the message of the Revelation with others and minister to them.

When God the Father gave the Revelation to Jesus Christ so that He could then show it to His servants, there was a sense of urgency. There were things which were to "shortly come to pass." With the passage of time, that sense of urgency has been lost to the Church, misunderstood, or misapplied, and replaced with interesting ideas. Historically, there are four basic views for interpreting the book of Revelation.

The Preterist view. The word preterist comes from a Latin word (*prater*) meaning "beyond," or "past." The partial Preterist would say that *most* of the Revelation has been fulfilled. The full (radical) Preterist would say that *all* of the Revelation has been fulfilled—including the Marriage Supper of the Lamb, the Great White Throne Judgment, and the New Heaven and New Earth. The Preterist view is grounded in the belief that the events relate to the destruction of Jerusalem in A.D. 70.

Another understanding of Revelation can be called the *Church Historical Approach.* The foundational thought is that the Revelation is a prophecy of the whole history of the Church, from the Ascension of Christ, to His Second Coming. At the time of the Reformation, this view was prominent among the Reformers. If this view is correct, an intriguing question arises: "In which chapter are we living?" If the Revelation is a prophecy of the history of the Church, then are Christians in chapter 13, chapter 17, or even chapter 20? Every age thinks they are "near the end." The Church in the current century is no exception. However, as a theological construct for interpreting the Revelation, the Church Historical Approach has lost popularity in favor of more sensational views.

The Futurist Approach says that the events of Revelation, from chapter 4 onward, concerns the future. With detailed charts and fanciful diagrams, there is a view of Revelation that follows current events and declares ancient prophecy is either currently being fulfilled, or is about to be fulfilled in the near future. The Futurists insist on taking the words of Revelation literally, in contrast to those who take the text spiritually.

The claim to be the "most literal" or "plain" of all the positions falls by the way side, for the Futurist, when it is pointed out that the events of the Revelation were to take place *soon*, according to verse 1. John was shown events that were to "shortly" come to pass. They were to happen soon, in John's time. It is hard to take the word in Revelation 1:1, "shortly" (Gk. *tachos*; a brief space [of time], i.e., in haste) literally, when more than 2,000 years have passed.

The Idealist Approach. A fourth school of thought for understanding Revelation is the Idealist, or Spiritual School. The idea is that Revelation is to be understood as a Present Blessing, as it sets forth great spiritual truths. The various symbols represent what will happen to the Church universal throughout the centuries until Jesus comes the Second Time. The details of the Revelation are not all in the past, nor are all the details in the future. The details of the Revelation do not reveal century by century what will happen in the life of the Church. Rather, the twenty-two chapters of the Revelation set forth in pictorial form what the Lord is doing in history. Undergirding the Present Blessing School of thought are the following concepts.

First, there is good, and there is evil. Evil is found in heaven in the form of fallen angels, one of which became the Dragon, Satan, that old Serpent, the Devil. Evil is found on earth in the form of the Beast from the Land, and the Beast from the Sea.

Second, there is a cosmic struggle between good and evil until the end of time. In heaven, Michael fought with the Devil in heaven, and prevailed. On earth, war is made against the saints by the Dragon, the Beast, and those who follow him. In the end, the church shall prevail.

Third, anyone who hurts the church will be destroyed. Any political entity, represented by the Beast from the Sea, and any religious entity that persecutes the church, represented by the Beast form the Land, shall be destroyed.

Fourth, one day there will be a new heaven and a new earth wherein righteousness dwells. Jesus Christ will be honored as King of kings and Lord of lords. The saints shall rule and reign with Him forever. There will be a New Jerusalem with new forms of worship. So, it is a glorious future that awaits the Church and all the saints who follow the Lamb.

2 Who bare record of the word of God, and of the testimony of Jesus Christ, and of all things that he saw.
3 Blessed *is* he that readeth, and they that hear the words of this prophecy, and keep those things which are written therein: for the time *is* at hand.

It is important to keep in mind that Biblical prophecy is not just about future events, but the message God has for His people. Biblical prophecy is telling forth spiritual truths. God has something to say to His people to help them in time of need.

It is also important that Revelation not be approached as a book that is a mystery, a puzzle, or something that cannot be understood. Daniel was told to seal up his vision, but John is told not to seal up the sayings of the prophecy of this book (Dan. 8:26; 12:4; Rev. 22:10).

Revelation is a book that has a blessing associated with it for those who hear, and keep those things which are written therein. This blessing provides the objective of the Revelation. It is to bless God's people, provided they hear, and do something specific.

What is to be heard?

The message that is to be heard is that God is sovereign over sin and suffering. The Lord reigns in heaven, and He rules the earth with a rod of iron.

What are those things written in the Revelation to be kept?

The faith of the saints is to be kept. No matter what happens, Christians are to follow the Lamb wherever He goes. They are to love the Lamb more than they love their own lives.

The unity of the Revelation must be kept in mind at all times, lest the distractions of obscure symbolism lead to fanciful interpretations that eventually dishonor the Lord. The Lord is dishonored when His Revelation is taken to scare people, or to make them fearful. "For God hath not given us the spirit of fear; but of power, and of love, and of a sound mind" (2 Tim. 1:7). In fact, the most frequent command in all of Scripture, given more than two hundred times, is this: Do not fear.

The time to not be afraid is *now,* in the present hour, for "the time is at hand." These words are repeated at the end of Revelation to indicate the unity of the Revelation, and to teach the Church that God is sovereign, and is always in control of both good and evil. "John, seal not the sayings of the prophecy of this book: for the time is at hand" (Rev. 22:10). When Daniel was told to seal up his vision, the events he was given were four hundred years in the future. The message John was given was an immediate reality to his generation, by interpretation, and then, the prophecy, timely to other generations, by way of application.

In 1 John 2:18, the author of the Revelation is even more emphatic. "Little children, it is the last time [hour]: and as ye have heard that antichrist shall come, even now are there many antichrists; whereby we know that it is the last time."

When people ask, "Are we living in the last days?" the Biblical answer is, "Yes!" There is no more prophecy that has to be fulfilled before Christ can return the Second Time for all who believe (Heb. 9:28). We are living in the last hour, the last day, the last time. Because this is true, there is a blessing for those who hear the Word of God, and are faithful to follow the Lamb.

Seven times throughout the Revelation, John pauses to say "Blessed are" (Rev. 1:3; 4:7; 14:13b; 16:15b; 19:9b; 20:6; 22:7, 14). Look for the blessings associated with the Revelation. If you want a blessing, do the following.

Read the Revelation. "Blessed is he that readeth, and they that hear the words of this prophecy, and keep those things which are written therein: for the time is at hand" (Rev. 1:3). While, "All scripture is given by inspiration of God, and is profitable for doctrine, for reproof, for correction, for instruction in righteousness" (2 Tim. 3:16), there is a special blessing associated with Revelation, because it teaches Christians about the place of suffering in the plan of God. There is the suffering of the righteous, and there is the suffering of the wicked. There are spiritual truths that can only be taught under pressure.

Die in the Lord. "And I heard a voice from heaven saying unto me, Write, Blessed are the dead which die in the Lord from henceforth: Yea, saith the Spirit, that they may rest from their labors; and their works do follow them" (Rev. 14:13).

Watch for the coming of the Lord, and walk in righteousness. "Behold, I come as a thief. Blessed is he that watcheth, and keepeth his garments, lest he walk naked, and they see his shame" (Rev. 16:15).

Respond to the gospel call to the Marriage Supper of the Lamb. "And he saith unto me, Write, Blessed are they which are called unto the marriage supper of the Lamb. And he saith unto me, These are the true sayings of God" (Rev. 19:9).

Take part in the First Resurrection. "Blessed and holy is he that hath part in the first resurrection: on such the second death hath no power, but they shall be priests of God and of Christ, and shall reign with him a thousand years" (Rev. 20:6).

Keep those things which are written in the Revelation. Take to heart the lessons of life God has conveyed to His people, and to the world, "for the time is at hand." "Behold, I come quickly: blessed is he that keepeth the sayings of the prophecy of this book" (Rev. 22:7).

Keep the Commandments. "Blessed are they that do his commandments, that they may have right to the tree of life, and may enter in through the gates into the city" (Rev. 22:14).

Look for the blessings associated with the Revelation.

The First Cycle

Suffering in the Plan of God for the Righteous

[4] John to the seven churches which are in Asia: Grace *be* unto you, and peace, from him which is, and which was, and which is to come; and from the seven Spirits which are before his throne;

Be Faithful

As a faithful apostle, John is writing to churches he was familiar with in Asia, in what is today, Turkey. He has a message for all who have been committed to his pastoral care.

John begins his message to the seven churches with a benediction, or a "good word." He has a Trinitarian blessing for God's people. The saints are to receive grace, or unmerited favor, and, they are to know the peace of God which passes all understanding. These gifts of divine mercy come from "He which is, which was, and which is to come." That is God the Father. While God exists now, He is the eternal one; He always was, and He always will be for "in him we live, and move, and have our being" (Acts 17:28).

These gifts of mercy come also from "the seven Spirits." That is God the Holy Spirit in all of His perfections. The symbolism means the Holy Spirit is complete. He is also compassionate, for the Spirit has the seven churches on His heart.

By understanding the symbolism used for the Holy Spirit, the realization comes that Biblical literalism is simply understanding what the author intended to say. If there is a failure in understanding the symbolism an author uses to convey truth, then there is a failure to read the text literally. When Jesus said

He was the Good Shepherd in John 10:11, He was not speaking without symbolism. Jesus was never literally a shepherd, for He was a carpenter by trade. However, the words of Jesus spoke a spiritual truth that can be understood. Jesus cares for His sheep.

Some Bible teachers will argue that a literal interpretation of Scripture means to take words of a text in their usual, or most basic sense, without metaphor, or allegory. When the Church of Rome took literally the words of Jesus to "eat" His body, and to "drink" His blood, the doctrine of transubstantiation was invented (Matt. 26:26–28). The world mocked, and spoke of Christians being cannibals.

Finally, the gifts of mercy also come from the resurrected Christ. Jesus is called the Faithful Witness, the First Begotten of the Dead, and the Prince of the Kings of the Earth. Jesus is also the Loving One.

5 **And from Jesus Christ, *who is* the faithful witness, *and* the first begotten of the dead, and the prince of the kings of the earth. Unto him that loved us, and washed us from our sins in his own blood,**

As a Prophet, Jesus is a faithful witness. As the Great High Priest, Jesus offered Himself as a sacrifice to wash us from our sins in His own blood. Jesus gave Himself for us in love. "He loves us," writes John. In the Greek, the word is in the present tense, not the past tense. A person can live forever in joy and happiness just knowing that Jesus loves them.

Jesus loves me, this I know,
  For the Bible tells me so;
Little ones to Him belong;
  They are weak, but He is strong.

Yes, Jesus loves me,
   Yes, Jesus loves me,
Yes, Jesus loves me,
   The Bible tells me so.

6 And hath made us kings and priests unto God and his
Father; to him *be* glory and dominion for ever and ever.
Amen.

Because Jesus is even now Prophet, Priest, and King, the heart of the Christian should, with John, break out in praise for Jesus has made us "kings and priests unto God. To Him be glory and dominion forever and ever. Amen."

7 Behold, he cometh with clouds; and every eye shall see
him, and they *also* which pierced him: and all kindreds of
the earth shall wail because of him. Even so, Amen.

One affirmation of truth leads to another. "Behold, He cometh." Jesus Christ is coming a Second Time for all who believe (Heb. 9:28). But before His Second Advent, Jesus will shake the earth in judgment, as individuals and nations discover in Revelation, and in every generation. Believe that, and say, "Amen."

8 I am Alpha and Omega, the beginning and the ending,
saith the Lord, which is, and which was, and which is to
come, the Almighty. 9 I John, who also am your brother,
and companion in tribulation, and in the kingdom and pa-
tience of Jesus Christ, was in the isle that is called Patmos,
for the word of God, and for the testimony of Jesus
Christ.

Though John was the beloved disciple, he still suffered for the cause and kingdom of Christ. Just because a person has tribulation does not mean he or she is loved less. John is still a citizen of the kingdom of heaven. He is a political prisoner on earth on the isle of Patmos, about 35 miles off the west coast of Asia, but he is free in Christ. The reason for John's political imprisonment was because he had received the Word of God, and bore testimony to Jesus Christ. John was willing to suffering any affliction for the cause of Christ. A. W. Pink notes, "Afflictions are light when compared with what we really deserve. They are light when compared with the sufferings of the Lord Jesus. But perhaps their real lightness is best seen by comparing them with the weight of glory which is awaiting us." John was about to look beyond time into eternity.

10 I was in the Spirit on the Lord's day, and heard behind me a great voice, as of a trumpet,

The Lord's Day is a *special* day, though in another context, as Paul writes, the Jewish fasts and feast days need not be honored. "One-man esteemeth one day above another: another esteemeth every day alike. Let every man be fully persuaded in his own mind" (Rom. 14:5). On the day of worship, according to the new Christian custom, John heard a great voice, which sounded like a trumpet.

11 Saying, I am Alpha and Omega, the first and the last: and, What thou seest, write in a book, and send *it* unto the seven churches which are in Asia; unto Ephesus, and unto Smyrna, and unto Pergamos, and unto Thyatira, and unto Sardis, and unto Philadelphia, and unto Laodicea.
12 And I turned to see the voice that spake with me. And being turned, I saw seven golden candlesticks;
13 And in the midst of the seven candlesticks *one* like unto the Son of

man, clothed with a garment down to the foot, and girt about the paps with a golden girdle.

When John turned to see the voice that spoke to him, he entered into the spiritual world, which reminds the Christian that there are physical eyes to see, and there are spiritual eyes to perceive spiritual truth. When the Holy Spirit opens our eyes to spiritual truths, we become like John, and like the servant of Elisha who saw only the armies of men until his spiritual eyes were opened.

> And when the servant of the man of God was risen early, and gone forth, behold, an host compassed the city both with horses and chariots. And his servant said unto him, Alas, my master! how shall we do? And he answered, Fear not: for they that be with us are more than they that be with them. And Elisha prayed, and said, Lord, I pray thee, open his eyes, that he may see. And the Lord opened the eyes of the young man; and he saw: and, behold, the mountain was full of horses and chariots of fire round about Elisha (2 Kgs. 6:14–17).

As John turns towards the voice that he heard, he saw the Heavenly Temple, for his eyes came upon seven golden candlesticks. And he saw the figure of the Son of man standing in the middle of the golden candlesticks.

In the Holy Temple, there was a Lampstand which represented Jesus as the light of the world. Jesus said, "I am the light of the world: he that followeth me shall not walk in darkness, but shall have the light of life" (John 8:12). Light is essential for life. Light dispels the darkness. It illuminates. It reveals objects for what they are. John saw Jesus in the midst of the seven churches, because Christ is in the midst of His people, wherever, and whoever they might be. Christ is always near His own.

14 His head and *his* hairs *were* white like wool, as white as snow; and his eyes *were* as a flame of fire;

The Bible tells us very little about the appearance of Jesus as a man. Isaiah the prophet predicted the Messiah would have "no form nor comeliness; [Heb. hadar; splendor] and when we shall see him, there is no beauty that we should desire Him" (Isa. 53:2). Like many Jews, Jesus had a beard, according to the prophet (Isa. 50:6). Many Christians are convinced the Shroud of Turin provides a portrait of Jesus, but that remains speculative. What is not speculative is the purity and power of the Lord Jesus.

The Glorified Christ

- CLOTHING: A full garment down to His feet with a golden sash around His chest
- HAIR: White as snow
- EYES: Flames of fire
- FEET: Burnished brass
- VOICE: A majestic sound of rushing water
- HAND: Seven stars were held in His right hand
- MOUTH: A sharp two-edged sword
- FACE: Like the shining of the sun

15 And his feet like unto fine brass, as if they burned in a furnace; and his voice as the sound of many waters.
16 And he had in his right hand seven stars: and out of his

mouth went a sharp two-edged sword: and his countenance *was* as the sun shineth in his strength.

The right hand is considered the hand of power and strength. It is mentioned seven times in the Revelation (Rev. 1:16, 17, 20; 2:1; 5:1, 7; 13:16). With His right-hand, Jesus holds the church secure (Rev. 1:16, 20; 2:1). With His right-hand, Jesus comforts His people (Rev. 1:17). With His right-hand, God holds a book on which is written His eternal decrees (Rev. 5:1) to give it to the Lamb (Rev. 5:7). The power and strength of God is imitated by the Beast of the Revelation (Rev. 13:16).

17 **And when I saw him, I fell at his feet as dead. And he laid his right hand upon me, saying unto me, Fear not; I am the first and the last:**

One of the testimonies for the deity of Christ is that He received worship. It is forbidden to worship nature (Exod. 20:3–5). The elect angels refuse to be worshipped (Rev. 19:10; 22:8). However, Jesus can be, and should be, worshipped as John does, along with the twenty-four elders (Rev. 5:8), and the four Living Creatures (Rev. 7:11).

The reason why Christians are not to fear is because Jesus is alive and in charge of life, and death. Time and again Jesus comes to His people to say, "Fear not," for the Good Shepherd knows how timid and fearful His sheep are by nature. Hear Jesus say to the Church, "Fear not, little flock; for it is your Father's good pleasure to give you the kingdom" (Luke 12:32). Hear Jesus say to John, "I am the First, and the Last."

18 **I *am* he that liveth, and was dead; and, behold, I am alive for evermore, Amen; and have the keys of hell and of**

death. [19] Write the things which thou hast seen, and the things which are, and the things which shall be hereafter;

A Scriptural Structure

- The Things Which John Has Seen
- The Things Which Are
- The Things Which Shall Soon Be Hereafter

[20] The mystery of the seven stars which thou sawest in my right hand, and the seven golden candlesticks. The seven stars are the angels of the seven churches: and the seven candlesticks which thou sawest are the seven churches.

Time and again throughout the Revelation, Scripture will interpret itself to identify the symbolism of the narrative. It is a foundational principle of hermeneutics to let the Bible explain itself, and then believe what is said. Here, John identifies the seven stars in the right hand of Jesus to be the angels of the seven churches.

Some Bible scholars believe the reference to the angels is a reference to the *ministers* of the seven churches. That may be a correct understanding, for the word angel does mean, literally, messenger. In addition, each of the letters of the Revelation is addressed "to the *angel* of" that congregation. The strong implication is that the letter is given to the *minister*, the pastoral leader of the local assembly.

However, it is also possible the seven angels refer to *guarding* angels. If this is correct, then every congregation has a *guarding* angel assigned to watch over the saints. This view has merit because elsewhere in the Revelation when angels are spoken of, there is no doubt that an angel is meant.

We know that Christians are to be careful to entertain strangers. "Be not forgetful to entertain strangers: for there by some have entertained angels unawares" (Heb. 13:2). We also know that angels are "sent forth to minister for them who shall be heirs of salvation" (Heb. 1:14). While the Lord does not need angels to guard churches, He does ordain they go forth. As the Creator, the Lord enjoys a variety of creatures, and employs them all in His service.

Without question, angels are not to be worshipped. Only the Lord God is to be worshipped and served (Matt. 4:9, 10). When we pray, we are to say, "Our Father, which art in heaven" (Matt. 6:9). Some angels are to be disbelieved, and that is, when they preach another gospel (Gal. 1:8, 9). But on the positive side, the presence of a guardian angel indicates the love and care of the Lord for His churches.

As the first chapter comes to a conclusion, a word of caution is offered to Bible students with over active imaginations. The temptation comes to create symbolism in Scripture where none exists. For example, it has been suggested that the seven churches represent seven church *ages.* There is nothing in Scripture to suggest such an idea; the dates given to each alleged age is arbitrary, and, if the Lord tarries, will have to be revised. Truth does not change.

Even worse, once people establish a cherished "System" of interpretation, they move from speculation to dogmatism. Evolution was popularized as a theory in 1859 with the publication of Charles Darwin's *On the Origin of the Species,* but today evolution is declared to be settled science. It is manifestly not, but that is the mantel of authority it has arrogated to itself.

In a large section of conservative Christendom, something similar has taken place. What began in the 1850s as "the blessed hope" for the soon return of Christ, has metamorphosed into a certainty that the signs of the time are now present, and the Church of Jesus Christ is living in the "Laodicean Age," an age of apostasy and failure. The theological "System" that advocates their elaborate and detailed view of the future is dogmatic, sensational, emotional, date setting, always wrong on important points, but never in doubt.

Revelation Chapter 2

The Church of Ephesus

1 Unto the angel of the church of Ephesus write; These things saith he that holdeth the seven stars in his right hand, who walketh in the midst of the seven golden candlesticks;

There are some common elements in the seven letters. In each letter, John is instructed to write and underscore the idea that it is Christ who is speaking to His churches. No person has a right to superimpose their own ideas on a congregation. Rather, we are "ambassadors for Christ" (2 Cor. 5:20). An ambassador conveys only the message that has been entrusted to him, and nothing more.

In each letter, Jesus identifies Himself. He is the One who holds the seven stars, and walks among the lampstands, so that He can say He will come and remove the lampstand if necessary.

In each letter, Jesus praises the good works that are done. Grace always precedes judgment.

In each letter, Jesus accuses the congregation of some transgression. The accusations are rooted in His intimate knowledge of the truth, so there can be no denial of what is being charged. The sins of the saints are real. Two churches are not charged with any transgression, the church in Philadelphia and the church in Smyrna.

In each letter, Jesus calls the church to repent, and exhorts them on how to live.

2 I know thy works, and thy labour, and thy patience, and how thou canst not bear them which are evil: and thou hast tried them which say they are apostles, and are not, and hast found them liars:

To each church the Lord says, "I know," and "I will." The Lord knows each church, and He knows that each church is not the same. The Lord will deal with each congregation individually. The primary way the Lord will *begin* to deal with the local assembly is by speaking to the "angel," or minister of the church. The Bible warns men not to be too eager to be a teacher in the church "My brethren, be not many masters, knowing that we shall receive the greater condemnation" (Jas. 3:1).

What the Lord knows about the church of Ephesus is commendable. He knows they are preforming good works. He knows they are laboring for His cause and kingdom. He knows they are being patient in a time of persecution and suffering. He knows the hearts of the saints are against those who are evil. The Lord knows the church has held individuals accountable who pretended to be apostles. Those individuals were found to be liars.

3 And hast borne, and hast patience, and for my name's sake hast laboured, and hast not fainted.

To emphasis His words of commendation, Jesus repeats the good He has witnessed in the church of Ephesus. The Lord knows the saints are patient, and are bearing up for His name's sake. The Lord knows the people have not fainted, become exhausted in kingdom work, or grown weary. He knows.

4 **Nevertheless I have *somewhat* against thee, because thou hast left thy first love.**

The word "nevertheless" is a transitional word. In context, it is a tragic word, because the transition is from commendation to condemnation. Despite all the good and positive facets of their ministry, the Lord has something against the people. He is very specific. The accusation is sharp, and painful. The people have left their first love.

Leaving the Lord as the first love of the heart will be the besetting sin in each church in Revelation which is confronted. This is the result of worldliness, and idolatry. When a congregation adopts the *standards* and practices of the world, and incorporates them in the assembly, the Lord notices. When a congregation accepts the *ideas* of the world, and brings them into worship, idolatry takes place. The God of revelation is replaced by various gods of men's imaginations, and love for the Lord is lost.

One modern day example is that of the Health and Wealth Gospel. It has caused many people to lose their true love for the Lord, for He is no longer worshipped and adored for who and what He is, but for what people think they can get out of Him. There is much talk about "seed faith." This spurious theology entices people to give "seed" money in order to manipulate God's grace and gifts. The Bible teaches that Christians are to give in order to be a blessing to others, and to glorify the Lord, not in order to be enriched personally. Jesus said, "It is more blessed to give than to receive" (Acts 20:35).

5 Remember therefore from whence thou art fallen, and repent, and do the first works; or else I will come unto thee quickly, and will remove thy candlestick out of his place, except thou repent.

The Divine solution for those who have lost their first love is to remember, repent, and repeat the first works of the faith. One of the first works of the faith, is to respond afresh to the love of Christ.

The word love is first used in Revelation 1:5b. "Unto him that loved [Gk. loves] us." It is a thrilling moment when a person realizes they are loved, and they have the capacity to love in return. Suddenly, love overshadows all else.

What Jesus was saying to the church of Ephesus, is that it is good the people were doctrinally sound, and bearing each day in a gracious manner. It was good that kingdom work was being accomplished. But love for Christ was most important of all. "Peter, do you love me?" asked Jesus. "Christian, do you love Jesus?" It is possible to become so passionate being an apologist for the Christian faith that we forget to love Jesus. The church at Ephesus hated the deeds of the Nicolaitanes. That was good. Jesus hated their deeds too.

6 But this thou hast, that thou hatest the deeds of the Nicolaitanes, which I also hate.

While hating the evil that men do, while maintaining doctrinal purity, while being discerning over apostolic leaders, individuals must not forget to love Jesus. That is the message to the church of Ephesus.

7 He that hath an ear, let him hear what the Spirit saith unto the churches; To him that overcometh will I give to

eat of the tree of life, which is in the midst of the paradise of God.

When a church has spiritual ears to hear what the Spirit says, the people will enjoy close fellowship with the Lord, symbolized by being given the right to eat of the Tree of Life, which is in the midst of the Paradise of God.

The Tree of Life is mentioned three times in Genesis (2:9; 2:22, 24), and four times in Revelation (2:7; 22:2, 14). Literally, the Tree of Life provided nourishment to Adam and Eve so they could enjoy fellowship with the Lord each evening in the cool of the day. Symbolically, in Revelation, that close fellowship is restored in the Paradise of God. God makes all things new for those who love Jesus. Paradise is restored, and fellowship with Him resumes.

The Letter to the Church in Smyrna

8 **And unto the angel of the church in Smyrna write; These things saith the first and the last, which was dead, and is alive;**

Smyrna was about 70 miles east of Ephesus. Like Ephesus, it was a real church, with an established congregation. What is unique about the church in Smyrna is that no charge is brought against the people. What John writes is an encouraging letter.

9 **I know thy works, and tribulation, and poverty, (but thou art rich) and *I know* the blasphemy of them which say they are Jews, and are not, but *are* the synagogue of Satan.**

The Bible presents three types of Jews. There is the ethnic Jew, referring to those who are descended from Abraham

(Matt. 3:9). There is the religious Jew, or proselyte to Judaism illustrated by Ruth. "And Ruth said, Intreat me not to leave thee, or to return from following after thee: for whither thou goest, I will go; and where thou lodgest, I will lodge: thy people shall be my people, and thy God my God" (Ruth 1:16). There is the regenerate Jew, meaning those who have the faith of Abraham and in his seed, the Lord Jesus. "Neither, because they are the seed of Abraham, are they all children: but, In Isaac shall thy seed be called" (Rom. 9:7). There is no anti-Semitism in Revelation, but there is a consistent teaching that the "true" Jew is the one who is "of faith." All who have the faith of the patriarch, "the same are the children of Abraham" (Gal. 3:7).

Those Jews who refuse to believe in Jesus as the Messiah, may *say* they are Jews, but when they come together in worship, they are actually a gathering (Gk. *sunagōgē*, an assemblage) of the disciples of Satan, and not as disciples of Jesus.

10 Fear none of those things which thou shalt suffer: behold, the devil shall cast *some* of you into prison, that ye may be tried; and ye shall have tribulation ten days: be thou faithful unto death, and I will give thee a crown of life.

The reference to enduring tribulation for ten days has led to speculation that the ten days is a veiled reference to ten *periods* of persecution.[1]

Others insist the ten days of Revelation 2:8 is a *literal* period of ten days of twenty-four hours for each day. Still others

[1] Ten primitive persecutions: (1) Nero, A.D. 67 (2) Domitian, A.D. 81 (3) Trajan, A.D. 108 (4) Marcus Aurelius Antoninus, A.D. 162 (5) Severus, A.D. 192 (6) Maximus, A.D. 235 (7) Decius, A.D. 249 (8) Valerian, A.D. 257 (9) Aurelian, A.D. 274 (10) Diocletian, A.D. 303.

believe the reference is *symbolic* for a short period of time. Uncertainty in understanding remains.

[11] **He that hath an ear, let him hear what the Spirit saith unto the churches; He that overcometh shall not be hurt of the second death.**

By allowing Scripture to explain itself, the meaning of the Second Death is set forth. "And death and hell were cast into the lake of fire. This is the second death" (Rev. 20:14). The Bible reveals who shall experience the Second Death. "But the fearful, and unbelieving, and the abominable, and murderers, and whoremongers, and sorcerers, and idolaters, and all liars, shall have their part in the lake which burneth with fire and brimstone: which is the second death" (Rev. 21:8). As fearful and terrible as the Second Death is, the faithful Christian shall overcome, and be victorious, and shall not be hurt by the judgment to come.

The larger message for the Church is that Christians *need* not to be afraid of the First Death, and they *need* not be afraid of persecution, for the soul shall not be hurt, but sheltered in the arms of God.

I feel the touch of hands so kind and gentle,
They're leading me in paths that I must trod;
I have no fear when Jesus walks beside me,
For I'm sheltered in the arms of God.

So let the storms rage high, the dark clouds rise,
They won't worry me for I'm sheltered safe within the arms of God;
He walks with me and naught of Earth can harm me,
Sheltered safe within the arms of God.

Soon I shall hear the call from Heavens portals,
Come home my child, it's the last mile you must trod;
Ill fall asleep and wake in God's new Heaven,
Sheltered safe within the arms of God.

So let the storms rage high, the dark clouds rise,
They won't worry me for I'm sheltered safe within the arms of God;

He walks with me and naught of Earth can harm me,
Sheltered safe within the arms of God.[2]

The Letter to the Church in Pergamos

12 And to the angel of the church in Pergamos write; These things saith he which hath the sharp sword with two edges;

Pergamum was an important city in the Roman Empire that sponsored a large temple to Zeus, who was portrayed as sitting on a throne. The presence of the pagan religion permeated society, and influenced the people economically and spiritually. The Church existed in the midst of great challenges, which is why Lord said, "I know where you live."

13 I know thy works, and where thou dwellest, *even* where Satans seat *is:* and thou holdest fast my name, and hast not denied my faith, even in those days wherein Antipas *was* my faithful martyr, who was slain among you, where Satan dwelleth.

The knowledge of the Lord concerning His people is extensive, and it is comforting. Sometimes Christians wonder if the

[2] Dottie Rambo.

Lord really cares what difficulties in life a person is suffering. The answer is that Jesus does know, and He does care.

Does Jesus care when my heart is pained
  Too deeply for mirth or song,
As the burdens press, and the cares distress,
  And the way grows weary and long?

Oh, yes, He cares, I know He cares,
  His heart is touched with my grief;
When the days are weary, the long nights dreary,
  I know my Savior cares.

Does Jesus care when my way is dark
  With a nameless dread and fear?
As the daylight fades into deep night shades,
  Does He care enough to be near?

Does Jesus care when I've tried and failed
  To resist some temptation strong;
When for my deep grief there is no relief,
  Though my tears flow all the night long?

Does Jesus care when I've said "goodbye"
  To the dearest on earth to me,
And my sad heart aches till it nearly breaks—
  Is it aught to Him? Does He see?[3]

14 But I have a few things against thee, because thou hast there them that hold the doctrine of Balaam, who taught Balac to cast a stumblingblock before the children

---

[3] Frank E. Graeff.

of Israel, to eat things sacrificed unto idols, and to commit fornication.

Because the Jewish community would be familiar with the narrative of the Old Testament Scriptures in Numbers 22—24, a reference is made to Balaam, who taught Balac how to get the children of Israel to commit idolatry, and engage in acts of sexual perversion. The attempt to corrupt the Church of God and lead Christians astray occurs in every generation, which is why Christians are exhorted to watch and to be vigilant. "Watch ye therefore, and pray always, that ye may be accounted worthy to escape all these things that shall come to pass, and to stand before the Son of man" (Luke 21:36).

[15] So hast thou also them that hold the doctrine of the Nicolaitanes, which thing I hate.

While the saints in the Church of Ephesus hated the deeds of the Nicolaitans, which the Lord Himself hated (Rev. 2:6), the Church of Pergamos held firmly to the Doctrine of the Nicolaitans. For the second time the Lord expressed His divine hatred (*miseō*, to detest).

[16] Repent; or else I will come unto thee quickly, and will fight against them with the sword of my mouth. [17] He that hath an ear, let him hear what the Spirit saith unto the churches; To him that overcometh will I give to eat of the hidden manna, and will give him a white stone, and in the stone a new name written, which no man knoweth saving he that receiveth *it*.

The reference to manna would remind the Jewish Christians how God is able to sustain His people who are faithful and trust in Him.

Guide me oh thou Great Jehovah,
Pilgrim through this barren land.
I am weak but thou are Mighty;
Hold me with thy powerful hand:
Bread of Heaven, Bread of Heaven
Feed me till I want no more;
Feed me till I want no more.[4]

Jesus Himself is the Bread of Heaven, "Then Jesus said unto them, Verily, verily, I say unto you, Moses gave you not that bread from heaven; but my Father giveth you the true bread from heaven" (John 6:32).

The reference to the white stone may speak of a jury practice in the ancient world whereby a person, in a court of law, was given a white stone if the jury members thought him to be innocent. The Lord will find individuals innocent who are faithful to Him in their heart and in their behavior.

Letter to the Church in Thyatira

18 And unto the angel of the church in Thyatira write; These things saith the Son of God, who hath his eyes like unto a flame of fire, and his feet *are* like fine brass;

To the Church in Thyatira, the Son of God reveals Himself as the one who searches out the behavior of the people with "eyes like unto a flame of fire." After an extensive examination and evaluation, the Son of God stands to judge individuals for "His feet are like fine brass." By administering judgment, the Lord stabilizes His Church, for feet of brass are firm. The gospel exhortation is for Christians to "stand fast in the Lord (1

[4] William Williams.

Thess. 3:8). Christians are not to be tossed about with every "wind and doctrine" (Eph. 4:14).

19 I know thy works, and charity, and service, and faith, and thy patience, and thy works; and the last *to be* more than the first.

The searching eyes of the Son of God finds much to commend. Five notable areas are recognized. The Church in Thyatira is to be commended for their record, their love, their service, their faithfulness, and their recent works. Now, as commendable as all of this is, there was serious sin in the assembly.

20 Notwithstanding I have a few things against thee, because thou sufferest that woman Jezebel, which calleth herself a prophetess, to teach and to seduce my servants to commit fornication, and to eat things sacrificed unto idols.

There was a teacher in the Church in Thyatira that was doing the destructive work of a Jezebel. As a result of her teaching, individuals felt comfortable enough to commit physical fornication, and to engage in acts of idolatry. The original Jezebel caused Israelites to worship Baal, and not Jehovah. Her spiritual descendent were just as wicked and treacherous.

The question of eating food sacrificed to idols was not a new issue for Jewish Christians. Paul dealt with the problem in his epistle to the Church in Corinth (1 Cor. 8:1–13). The apostles conclusion, that while food offered to an idol was a foolish act for an idol is nothing. Nevertheless, in order not to offend a weaker brother in the faith, restraint was recommended, though total prohibition was not. In Revelation, the Church in Thyatira was condemned for lack of any sympathy to a weaker brother which allowed bold behavior in a questionable area.

21 And I gave her space to repent of her fornication; and
she repented not. 22 Behold, I will cast her into a bed, and
them that commit adultery with her into great tribulation,
except they repent of their deeds. 23 And I will kill her
children with death; and all the churches shall know that I
am he which searcheth the reins and hearts: and I will give
unto every one of you according to your works.

For those who do not repent, and forsake the teachings of Jezebel, the Lord says He will personally "kill her children with death." The children refer to the followers of this false teacher.

24 But unto you I say, and unto the rest in Thyatira, as many as have not this doctrine, and which have not known the depths of Satan, as they speak; I will put upon you none other burden.

One way that many people in the Church become ensnared with false doctrine, is by seeking out deeper spiritual truths, called here, "the depths of Satan." The Mormons appeal to many people in the established Christian church by suggesting they have something more to offer in the Book of Mormon.

The Prophet Joseph Smith, who "translated" the Book of Mormon stated in its Introduction, "I told the brethren that the Book of Mormon was the most correct of any book on earth, and the keystone of our religion, and a man would get nearer to God by abiding by its precepts, than by any other book." The Seventh Day Adventist, the Christian Science, and many other cults attract followers by appealing to a natural curiosity for deeper knowledge of spiritual matters.

The Church must remember that it already has a sure word of prophecy, and simply need to contend for the faith once delivered to it.

It is possible that in the Church of Thyatira "that woman Jezebel" was teaching people they were free from conventual restrictions. They were free to commit acts of immorality. They were free to honor false gods. They were free in Christ, for, did not Paul say that "the law of the Spirit of life in Christ Jesus hath made me free from the law of sin and death?" Paul had much to say about freedom, and so did Peter. Peter said, "As free, and not using your liberties for a cloak of maliciousness, but as the servants of God" (1 Pet. 2:16).

25 **But that which ye have *already* hold fast till I come.**

As Christ confronts His people, it is seen that the local assembly was divided. While many of the saints were faithful, some where holding to harmful doctrine. The church was in danger of losing its lampstand, though not all would be extinguished. Some would be faithful, victorious, and overcome the temptation to depart from the faith once delivered to the saints.

26 **And he that overcometh, and keepeth my works unto the end, to him will I give power over the nations:**

For those who are faithful, the Lord promises to "give power over the nations."

27 **And he shall rule them with a rod of iron; as the vessels of a potter shall they be broken to shivers: even as I received of my Father.**

As King of kings and Lord of lords, Jesus is the Prince, or Ruler of all the kings of the earth. The world today is not being run by the United Nations, nor the president of any country, or a parliamentary official. King Jesus is ruling the nations with a rod of iron. The worldwide Coronavirus Pandemic of 2020 should dispel any doubt to the contrary. Within a few short days, the exalted Lord of Glory shook the nations on the earth, and made them tremble. Irrational fear and unimaginable terror filled the hearts of the leaders, and the world. In every generation, in every century, Jesus rules with a rod of iron.

The allusion is to Psalm 2:9. It was said of the Messiah, "Thou shalt break them with a rod of iron; thou shalt dash them in pieces like a potters vessel." There is a terrible judgment associated with the person and work of Jesus Christ. The only way to stand in the Day of Judgment is to stand in Christ.

A wonderful Savior is Jesus my Lord,
  a wonderful Savior to me;
He hideth my soul in the cleft of the rock,
  where rivers of pleasure I see.

He hideth my soul in the cleft of the rock
  that shadows a dry, thirsty land;
He hideth my life in the depths of His love,
  and covers me there with His hand,
  and covers me there with His hand.[5]

28 And I will give him the morning star.

The promise made to the Church of Thyatira, is that they would be given the morning star if they were faithful. In Revelation 22:16 Christ is said to be the bright morning star. "I Jesus have sent mine angel to testify unto you these things in the churches. I am the root and the offspring of David, and the bright and morning star" (Rev. 22:16). The victor will have Christ himself.

---

[5] Fanny Crosby.

29 He that hath an ear, let him hear what the Spirit saith unto the churches.

Revelation Chapter 3

The Letter to the Church in Sardis

1 **And unto the angel of the church in Sardis write; These things saith he that hath the seven Spirits of God, and the seven stars; I know thy works, that thou hast a name that thou livest, and art dead.**

The Lord has some immediate and harsh words for the Church in Sardis. It is a sleepy church and needs to wake up, become watchful, and strengthen specific spiritual areas that have been neglected.

2 **Be watchful, and strengthen the things which remain,**
that are ready to die: for I have not found thy works per-
fect before God.
3 **Remember therefore how thou hast re-**
ceived and heard, and hold fast, and repent. If therefore
thou shalt not watch, I will come on thee as a thief, and
thou shalt not know what hour I will come upon thee.

The road to spiritual recovery is rooted in remembering what has been received and heard, resolving to protect the faith, and repenting, by having an authentic change of beliefs and behavior. If this is not done, the Lord will come as a thief, in an hour that is unexpected, and judge the church.

[4] **Thou hast a few names even in Sardis which have not defiled their garments; and they shall walk with me in white: for they are worthy.**

The harsh words of the Lord were not directed at everyone indiscriminately. The Lord knew there were some in Sardis who were holy. There were individuals walking in the Lord with a clear conscience. They were dressed in white, a symbol of purity and holiness. There were some who were worthy of commendation and honor. The people were worthy, because Jesus made them worthy. They were dressed in white, because they had been given new clothes.

[5] **He that overcometh, the same shall be clothed in white raiment; and I will not blot out his name out of the book of life, but I will confess his name before my Father, and before his angels.**

The allusion may be to a portion of an imprecatory prayer in Psalm 69. "Let them be blotted out of the book of the living, and not be written with the righteous" (v. 28). The idea is that those who live a victorious life for Christ will be honored. They have not broken covenant with God. They have confessed the name of Jesus, and so the Lord will confess their name in heaven. Here are words of encouragement and blessing.

[6] **He that hath an ear, let him hear what the Spirit saith unto the churches.**

The Letter to the Church in Philadelphia

[7] **And to the angel of the church in Philadelphia write; These things saith he that is holy, he that is true, he that**

hath the key of David, he that openeth, and no man shutteth; and shutteth, and no man openeth;

It is an encouraging letter that is written to the Church in Philadelphia. It is a letter free of condemnation and judgment. It is a letter written by the One who is holy and is true. It is a letter written by the One who fulfills prophecy. In Isaiah 22:22 the prophet tells the palace administrator that he will be replaced by Eliakim, a type of the Messiah, for God "will place on his shoulder the key to the house of David." The one who holds the keys has the authority. As the greater son of David, Jesus has been given control and authority over his domain, indeed over heaven and earth itself (Matt. 28:18).

8 **I know thy works: behold, I have set before thee an open door, and no man can shut it: for thou hast a little strength, and hast kept my word, and hast not denied my name.**

The Church in Philadelphia may have been a small congregation, for it is said to have only a little strength. Nevertheless, the church is known to the Lord, and is significant to Him. He who has the Key of David knows how to unlock a door of great opportunity of service for the church, which no man is able to close. The people have kept the word of the Lord, and not denied Christ. Such faithfulness attracted the attention of the Lord of glory, and is to be rewarded.

9 **Behold, I will make them of the synagogue of Satan, which say they are Jews, and are not, but do lie; behold, I will make them to come and worship before thy feet, and to know that I have loved thee.**

One way the Lord said He would honor the Church in Philadelphia was to make those individuals in the Church of

Smyrna, who assembled as the people of Satan, submit to their authority. The people would know how much the Lord loves the Church in Philadelphia.

[10] Because thou hast kept the word of my patience, I also will keep thee from the hour of temptation, which shall come upon all the world, to try them that dwell upon the earth.

When the Lord said He would keep the *first* century Church in Philadelphia from a coming hour, or period of temptation (Gk. *peirasmos* [pi-ras-mos], testing), there is no need to read into the text a meaning that supports a particular bias. The hour of temptation, the hour of testing is coming to try "them that dwell upon the earth," a reference to those who do not believe in Jesus.

Unbelievers are
"Those Who Dwell on the Earth"

- Revelation 3:10
- Revelation 6:10
- Revelation 11:10
- Revelation 13:8
- Revelation 13:14
- Revelation 14:6
- Revelation 17:8

Believers are Those who
"Dwell in Heaven"

"And hath raised us up together,
and made us sit together in heavenly places in Christ Jesus"
Ephesians 2:6

- Revelation 12:12
- Revelation 13:6
- Revelation 21:3

The Lord would keep (Gk. *tēreō* [tay-reh-o]; to guard from loss or injury), the Lord would preserve the Church in Philadelphia, not by removal, and not by rapture, but by keeping an eye on the people Himself. As Noah and his family were kept from the hour of trial that came upon those who dwelt on the earth in his day, so the Church in Philadelphia would be kept by the power of God. The hour of trouble is coming on the unbelievers. The hour of trouble is coming upon the worldly.

11 **Behold, I come quickly: hold that fast which thou hast, that no man take thy crown.** 12 **Him that overcometh will I make a pillar in the temple of my God, and he shall go no more out: and I will write upon him the name of my God, and the name of the city of my God, *which is* new Jerusalem, which cometh down out of heaven from my God: and *I will write upon him* my new name.**

To be a *pillar* in the Temple of God is to be an object of grace and beauty, while serving an important supporting function. That would be an encouraging thought for Christians struggling to be faithful in a small church. Every believer should seek to be a pillar in the Temple of God, which is said to exist in heaven.

13 **He that hath an ear, let him hear what the Spirit saith unto the churches.**

Part of the message the Spirit would have the churches to hear is that the Jewish branches were broken off, that Gentiles might be grafted in (Rom. 11:19). "For I would not, brethren, that ye should be ignorant of this mystery, lest ye should be wise in your own conceits; that blindness in part is happened to Israel, until the fulness of the Gentiles be come in" (Rom. 11:25).

The Letter to the Church of the Laodiceans

14 And unto the angel of the church of the Laodiceans write; These things saith the Amen, the faithful and true witness, the beginning of the creation of God; 15 I know thy works, that thou art neither cold nor hot: I would thou wert cold or hot. 16 So then because thou art lukewarm, and neither cold nor hot, I will spue thee out of my mouth. 17 Because thou sayest, I am rich, and increased with goods, and have need of nothing; and knowest not that thou art wretched, and miserable, and poor, and blind, and naked:

Historically, the people in the city of Laodicea were known to be very proud of their great wealth derived from a strong banking system, a textile industry, and the medicine that was made. This is significant, because the Lord will accuse the Church of the Laodiceans of being poor, naked, and blind. What the Church gloried in physically, was overshadowed by their true spiritual state. The Church was *not* rich towards God, it was *not* clothed in garments of righteousness, and it *was* sick. There was no joy in the Lord. The people were wretched and miserable in their souls. They were to be pitied, not praised.

18 I counsel thee to buy of me gold tried in the fire, that thou mayest be rich; and white raiment, that thou mayest

be clothed, and *that* the shame of thy nakedness do not appear; and anoint thine eyes with eyesalve, that thou mayest see.

If the people repented according to gospel terms, the Lord promised to give the Church pure gold, gold tried in the fire, that they might be truly rich in spiritual matters. Bankers, take notice of this spiritual truth. Textile workers, listen. I will give you white raiment that you may be clothed. And pharmacy workers, I will give you something to anoint your eyes that you may clearly see spiritual truths.

19 As many as I love, I rebuke and chasten: be zealous
therefore, and repent. 20 Behold, I stand at the door, and
knock: if any man hear my voice, and open the door, I will come in to him, and will sup with him, and he with me.

The door of the Church in Philadelphia was open, but the door in the Church of the Laodiceans was shut. It is possible for a Church to close itself off against Jesus. It was amazing the Lord did not give up on the congregation. Rather, He waited patiently to have fellowship with them. The message is clear. Christians are responsible to repent. Christians are responsible to hear the Lord's voice, and what the Spirit has to say to the churches. Christians are responsible to seek to have fellowship with the Lord of Glory. Let those who have spiritual ears hear Christ knocking at the door.

21 To him that overcometh will I grant to sit with me in
my throne, even as I also overcame, and am set down with
my Father in his throne. 22 He that hath an ear, let him
hear what the Spirit saith unto the churches.

The First Cycle with its Seven Sections consisting of Seven Letters to the Seven Churches of Asia ends with a familiar word of exhortation. May what the Spirit has to say to the churches be heard for the good of Christians, and for the glory of the Lord.

Revelation Chapter 4

THE SECOND CYCLE (4:1—8:1)

Introduction to the Seven Seals

[1] After this I looked, and, behold, a door *was* opened in heaven: and the first voice which I heard *was* as it were of a trumpet talking with me; which said, Come up hither, and I will shew thee things which must be hereafter.

As the Second Cycle with Seven Sections consisting of Seven Seals begins, John sees a door opened in heaven. The heart of the Christian remembers that Jesus said of Himself, "I am the door: by me if any man enters in, he shall be saved, and shall go in and out, and find pasture" (John 10:9).

When John looked and beheld a door opened in heaven, he was *not* experiencing a radical break from the vision images in chapters one and two. The image of the glorified Christ took place in heaven, while John was "in the Spirit" (Rev. 1:10). The vision continued, for John noticed something else in his exalted state. There was a door in heaven.

The Doors of the Revelation	
• The Open Door in Philadelphia	Revelation 3:8
• The Closed Door in Laodicea	Revelation 3:20

• The Open Door in Heaven	Revelation 4:1
"Come Hither"	
• Come and see things hereafter	Revelation 4:1
• Come and see the judgement of the great whore	Revelation 17:1
• Come and see the bride, the Lamb's Wife	Revelation 21:9

Other than noticing there was a door, John moved on to comment on a voice he heard in heaven. The voice had, to him, the sound of a trumpet. The voice spoke to John directly, and said, "Come up hither [here], and I will shew thee things which must be hereafter." As a result of the summons, John said he was once more immediately "in the spirit."

2 And immediately I was in the spirit: and, behold, a throne was set in heaven, and *one* sat on the throne.

Seeing God in Color

3 And he that sat was to look upon like a jasper and a sardine stone: and *there was* a rainbow round about the throne, in sight like unto an emerald.

Because no man can see God and live (Exod. 33:20), John is given a portrait of the majestic beauty and glory of God. Precious gems are brought forth: jasper (with brown, yellow, or reddish colors), sardine (blood red), an emerald (green), and all the colors of the rainbow: violet, indigo, blue, green, yellow, orange, and red.

Twenty-Four Elders

4 And round about the throne *were* four and twenty seats: and upon the seats I saw four and twenty elders sitting, clothed in white raiment; and they had on their heads crowns of gold.

Around a central throne in heaven, John sees twenty-four other thrones on which are seated twenty-four elders clothed in white, with crowns of gold on their heads. The garments speak of purity and the robe of righteousness which God gives to those who are saved. The crowns of gold speak of the right to rule. The Church is reminded that Christ has made us kings and priests unto our God (Rev. 1:6). Those seated on the thrones are kings, they are conquerors who reign with the Lord.

Who are the twenty-four elders? They may represent all the redeemed of the Old Testament saints and New Testament saints. The number twenty-four itself is found elsewhere in the Revelation as the twelve tribes of Israel, and the twelve apostles, united in the New Jerusalem (Rev. 21:12, 13).

Part of the character of God is that He enjoys a relationship with others. Some of those who have a relationship with God are heavenly creatures, who appear to be very strange to the human mind. Some are angels. Some are humans. God does not need a relationship with others, but He is pleased to create and relate to His creation.

The Seven Spirits of God

[5] And out of the throne proceeded lightnings and thunderings and voices: and *there were* seven lamps of fire burning before the throne, which are the seven Spirits of God.

God is spirit, and has no form, so attention is paid to His beauty, and power, represented by thunder and lightning. Also present are seven burning torches, which are the seven Spirits of God. Here is a symbol of a symbol. Seven torches are said to represent the seven spirits, which represents the one Spirit.

Four Living Creatures

[6] And before the throne *there was* a sea of glass like unto crystal: and in the midst of the throne, and round about the throne, *were* four beasts full of eyes before and behind.

The Living Creatures are magnificent heavenly beings. They have the ability to move with great speed, reflected in their six wings, and they have vast knowledge, indicated by having many eyes.

The image of the Four Beasts, or Four Living Creatures, would remind the Churches of the creatures Ezekiel saw (Ezekiel 1:5–14). If there is interest in these creatures, who may represent the various orders of angels in heaven, attention should be given to the writings of Thomas Aquarius (c. 1225–1274), an Italian Dominican friar. Thomas is called the Angelic Doctor, because he wrote so much about angels.

[7] And the first beast *was* like a lion, and the second beast like a calf, and the third beast had a face as a man, and the fourth beast *was* like a flying eagle.

Four Living Creatures
• FIRST: Lion / Six wings / Full of eyes / Holy! Holy! Holy!
• SECOND: Calf / Six wings / Full of eyes / Holy! Holy! Holy!
• THIRD: Man/ Six wings / Full of eyes / Holy! Holy! Holy!
• FOURTH: Eagle / Six wings / Full of eyes / Holy! Holy! Holy!

8 **And the four beasts had each of them six wings about *him;* and *they were* full of eyes within: and they rest not day and night, saying, Holy, holy, holy, Lord God Almighty, which was, and is, and is to come.**

In Isaiah 6, the angels sing unto the Lord, calling out to one another, "Holy, holy, holy, is the Lord of hosts: the whole earth is full of his glory."

In the Revelation, the angels sing night and day, and say, "Holy, holy, holy, Lord God Almighty, which was, and is, and is to come."

A Song of Creation

9 **And when those beasts give glory and honour and thanks to him that sat on the throne, who liveth for ever**
and ever, 10 The four and twenty elders fall down before him that sat on the throne, and worship him that liveth for ever and ever, and cast their crowns before the throne, say-
ing, 11 Thou art worthy, O Lord, to receive glory and honour and power: for thou hast created all things, and for thy pleasure they are and were created.

While Jesus is the Savior of souls, it must not be forgotten that He is the Creator. The Twenty-four Elders unite with the

Four Living Creatures to honor Christ as Creator. Join now in singing the first song, the Song of Creation.

> Thou art worthy,
> O Lord, to receive glory and honour and power:
> for thou hast created all things,
> and for thy pleasure they are and were created.

Revelation Chapter 5

Still in the Heavenly Temple

A Scroll of Great Significance In the Right Hand of the One who Sat on the Throne

1 And I saw in the right hand of him that sat on the throne a book written within and on the backside, sealed with seven seals.

The "right hand" of God is an anthropomorphism, or symbolic representation of God. God is a Spirit; and they that worship Him must worship in spirit and in truth" (John 4:24). The right hand is the place of privilege, honor, and power. In the right hand of the One who sat on the throne was a book, or scroll of history, written on both sides for the decrees of God are detailed, complete, and certain. The scroll was sealed with seven seals.

A Strong Angel

2 And I saw a strong angel proclaiming with a loud voice, Who is worthy to open the book, and to loose the seals thereof?

Not only was John anxious to see history inscrolled, or unraveled, so are the angels. Peter spoke of how the angels desire to look into the things which pertain to salvation (1 Pet. 1:2). "Unto whom it was revealed, that not unto themselves, but unto us they did minister the things, which are now reported unto you by them that have preached the gospel unto you with the Holy Ghost sent down from heaven; which things the angels desire to look into."

3 And no man in heaven, nor in earth, neither under the earth, was able to open the book, neither to look thereon.

It must not be thought that individuals were brought forth to be evaluated for worthiness to open the seven seals. Rather, John immediately perceived that in all creation, no one is worthy to open the book, or to read with complete understanding the history that was on the scroll. This is because, "The secret things belong unto the Lord our God: but those things which are revealed belong unto us and to our children for ever, that we may do all the words of this law" (Deut. 29:29).

4 And I wept much, because no man was found worthy to open and to read the book, neither to look thereon.

John wept over the tragic idea that no one was found worthy to open, to read, or to look with understanding what God has decreed shall come to pass.

A Talking Elder

5 And one of the elders saith unto me, Weep not: behold, the Lion of the tribe of Juda, the Root of David, hath prevailed to open the book, and to loose the seven seals thereof.

While still in his grief, an elder came to console John. John, weep not, for someone is worthy to open the book, and to loosen the seven seals. That someone is the Lion of the Tribe of Judah. He is the Root of David. He is the one who has conquered. He is the one who has prevailed (Gk. *nikaō*; to subdue [literally or figurative]). Jesus has subdued the Devil, sin, death, the grave, and the demons of hell. How marvelous is this Lion, a symbol of power and strength. How glorious is this Root of David, for He is the promised Messiah, and He is wise. He has power to open the book, and He has wisdom to understand what He looks upon and reads.

A Sacrificial Lamb

6 **And I beheld, and, lo, in the midst of the throne and of the four beasts, and in the midst of the elders, stood a Lamb as it had been slain, having seven horns and seven eyes, which are the seven Spirits of God sent forth into all the earth.**

When John turned to behold, or gaze upon the Lion of the Tribe of Judah, when John turned to see the Root of David, he was amazed. Lo! John saw in the middle of the high seat of the throne, in the middle of the Four Living Creatures, in the middle of the Twenty-four Elders, a Lamb which appeared to have been put to death, for it was bloody. The Lamb was very unusual, for it had seven horns protruding from its head, and seven eyes. John understood the eyes to be symbolic of the seven Spirits of God, sent out into all the earth.

The meaning of the symbolism is not difficult for a Christian to discern. Instead of a Lion that conquers, John sees a

Lamb. This is the paradox found in the spiritual realm. True strength is found in weakness. Life is found in death. The Lion is the Lamb. The Conquest is Death. The Root of David is the Tree of Life. The Lamb that looked as if it had been sacrificed, by having its throat cut resulting in a bloodletting, is alive, having seven horns and seven eyes.

The Lamb has power, for horns are a sign of power in the Bible. The Lamb has complete wisdom for it has seven eyes which sees everything perfectly. The Lamb also has the seven Spirits of God, which are sent forth into all the earth. It is the Lamb who sends forth the Spirit in all of His ministry perfections. "And the spirit of the Lord shall rest upon him, the spirit of wisdom and understanding, the spirit of counsel and might, the spirit of knowledge and of the fear of the Lord" (Isa. 11:2).

7 And he came and took the book out of the right hand of him that sat upon the throne. 8 And when he had taken the book, the four beasts and four *and* twenty elders fell down before the Lamb, having every one of them harps, and golden vials full of odours, which are the prayers of saints.

Here is another affirmation to the divinity of Christ, for as soon as the Lion of the Tribe of Judah, the Root of the Branch of David, the Sacrificial Lamb takes the scroll out of the right hand of the One who sat on the throne, He is worshipped. The Living Creatures of Heaven worship Jesus. The Twenty-four Elders worship Jesus. With musical harps and bowls filled with sweet-smelling prayers, Jesus is worshipped.

Concerning the prayers of saints, they are said to be a sweet-smelling odor to God. If ever there was time when the Church needed to pray, it is now. E. M. Bounds, in his *Power*

Through Prayer, noted, "What the Church needs today is not more machinery, or better, not new organizations, or more and novel methods, but men whom the Holy Ghost can use, men of prayer, men mighty in prayer. The Holy Ghost does not flow through methods, but men. He does not come on machinery, but on men. He does not anoint plans, but men, men of prayer."

A New Song of Salvation

**9 And they sung a new song, saying, Thou art worthy to
take the book, and to open the seals thereof: for thou wast
slain, and hast redeemed us to God by thy blood out of
every kindred, and tongue, and people, and nation; 10 And
hast made us unto our God kings and priests: and we shall
reign on the earth.**

Jesus is worthy because He died to redeem with His precious blood His own from every tribe and tongue on earth. Because of Christ's great work of redemption, Christians are made kings and priests to reign on the earth. This is the second time the churches are told they are kings and priests. In Revelation 1 we read, "And hath made us kings and priests unto God and his Father; to him be glory and dominion for ever and ever. Amen" (Rev. 1:6). The "us" of Revelation refers to all believers, Jews and Gentiles, united together in one kingdom. There is no Jewish kingdom and a Gentile kingdom forever. There is only the one Kingdom of God. No one is replaced. No one is displaced. All are equal in the Kingdom of Heaven. Therefore, let all the saints sing together with one voice and in one accord a new song.

Thou art worthy to take the book,
and to open the seals thereof:
for thou wast slain,
and hast redeemed us to God by thy blood
out of every kindred, and tongue, and people, and nation;
And hast made us unto our God kings and priests:
and we shall reign on the earth.

11 And I beheld, and I heard the voice of many angels round about the throne and the beasts and the elders: and the number of them was ten thousand times ten thousand, and thousands of thousands;

Ten thousand times ten thousand (100,000,000) is a term of completion, and indicates that angels, along with the Living Creatures of heaven, and the Twenty-four elders sing a new song unto the Lord. There is a great cacophony of sight and sound of worship and praise.

12 Saying with a loud voice, Worthy is the Lamb that was slain to receive power, and riches, and wisdom, and strength, and honour, and glory, and blessing.

In this new song, attention is drawn to the Lamb, an image which is highlighted in Revelation twenty-eight times. However, outside the book of Revelation, the image of Christ as the Lamb of God is not frequently found (John 1:29, 36; Acts 8:32; 1 Pet. 1:19). It is John in particular who wants to convey Jesus as the Lamb, and unite Him to the symbolism of the Old Testament sacrifices.

Jesus is worthy to receive power. He is worthy to receive all the riches of the universe, tangible and intangible. Christ is worthy to receive all wisdom, human and divine. He is worthy to receive the strength of omnipotence. He is worthy of honor. Jesus is worthy of glory. He is worthy of being blessed. "Worthy is the Lamb that was slain to receive power, and riches, and wisdom, and strength, and honour, and glory, and blessing."

[13] **And every creature which is in heaven, and on the earth, and under the earth, and such as are in the sea, and all that are in them, heard I saying, Blessing, and honour, and glory, and power, *be* unto him that sitteth upon the throne, and unto the Lamb for ever and ever.**

Because He is worthy, because Jesus obeyed the Father, because the Father was well pleased with His Son, Jesus does receive the acclamation of all creation. "Blessing, and honour, and glory, and power, be unto him that sitteth upon the throne, and unto the Lamb for ever and ever."

[14] **And the four beasts said, Amen. And the four *and* twenty elders fell down and worshipped him that liveth for ever and ever.**

The worship of Jesus shall never cease. It shall last for ever and ever. Let the church join in endless praise.

I will extol thee, my God, O king;
and I will bless thy name for ever and ever.
Every day will I bless thee;
and I will praise thy name for ever and ever.

Great is the Lord, and greatly to be praised;
and his greatness is unsearchable.
One generation shall praise thy works to another,
and shall declare thy mighty acts.

—Psalm 145:1–4

Revelation Chapter 6

The Seven Seals are Opened

The First Seal: A Rider on a White Horse: Conquest

1 **And I saw when the Lamb opened one of the seals, and I heard, as it were the noise of thunder, one of the four beasts saying, Come and see.**

With the glory of heaven in his mind, and the song of praise to the Lamb ringing in his ears, John's attention is redirected. John is commanded to come and see the Four Horsemen of the Apocalypse Ride across the earth. John will behold the present reality of life. As wonderful as heaven is, life on earth is terrible. There is no place to run or hide for the average person. It is a fragile life on earth. This is an evil world we live in now. Though presented sequentially, all this happens concurrently. First the suffering, then the glory.

2 **And I saw, and behold a white horse: and he that sat on him had a bow; and a crown was given unto him: and he went forth conquering, and to conquer.**

When the First Seal was opened, John saw a majestic Rider on a White Horse. To him was given a crown, and he went forth conquering.

Though Jesus is honored and praised as being worthy, though Jesus is sovereignly in control, though Jesus is unrolling the scroll of history, what unfolds is a terrifying picture. Four Horsemen are riding, leaving behind a trail of death and destruction. There is no peace and prosperity. There is conquest, war, famine, and death.

The Second Seal: The Rider on the Red Horse: War

3 And when he had opened the second seal, I heard the
second beast say, Come and see. 4 And there went out an-
other horse *that was* red: and *power* was given to him that
sat thereon to take peace from the earth, and that they
should kill one another: and there was given unto him a
great sword.

When the Second Seal was opened, John saw a Red Horse. The Rider on the Red Horse was given a great sword and power to take peace from the earth. As a result, people killed one another.

The Third Seal: The Rider on the Black Horse: Famine

5 And when he had opened the third seal, I heard the
third beast say, Come and see. And I beheld, and lo a black
horse; and he that sat on him had a pair of balances in his
hand. 6 And I heard a voice in the midst of the four beasts
say, A measure of wheat for a penny, and three measures of
barley for a penny; and *see* thou hurt not the oil and the
wine.

When the Third Seal was opened, John saw a Black Horse. The Rider on the Black Horse had a pair of scales in his hand to measure out food. The oil and wine were not to be harmed.

The Fourth Seal: The Rider on the Pale-Green Horse: Death

7 And when he had opened the fourth seal, I heard the
voice of the fourth beast say, Come and see. 8 And I
looked, and behold a pale horse: and his name that sat on him was Death, and Hell followed with him. And power was given unto them over the fourth part of the earth, to kill with sword, and with hunger, and with death, and with the beasts of the earth.

When John saw the Fourth Seal opened, he saw a Pale-Green Horse. The Rider on the Pale-Green Horse was being followed by Death and Hell. Power was given to the Rider on the Pale-Green Horse over one fourth of the earth, resulting in slaughter with the sword, hunger, death, and attacks by animals.

While much speculation surrounds the identity of the Four Horsemen and what they each represent, a correct understanding of the vision is that of life. Every generation knows individuals who want to conquer others by political, economic, or military means. Every generation knows the ravages of war. Every generation struggles with hunger, and death. The church in every generation will experience, first the suffering, then the glory.

The Fifth Seal: The Souls under the Altar

9 And when he had opened the fifth seal, I saw under the altar the souls of them that were slain for the word of God, and for the testimony which they held:

In the first four seals the sufferings on earth are viewed. In the Fifth Seal attention is returned to heaven. Time and again in the Revelation there will be this flowing movement from earth (Rev. 1:9), to heaven (Rev. 1:10–20), to earth (Rev. 2:1—3:22), to heaven (Rev. 4:1—5:14), to earth again (Rev. 6:1–8), and then to heaven (Rev. 6:9ff) etc. In heaven, John sees the altar. Under the altar John beheld the souls of martyred saints. They were killed for the Word of God, and for their personal testimony they confessed before a hostile world. They were killed willingly. As Jim Elliot, "He is no fool who gives what he cannot keep to gain that which he cannot lose." At age 28, Jim Elliot gave his life for Christ along the Curaray River, Ecuador in an attempt to evangelize the Huaorani people. When that attempt failed, he went through gates of splendor to be numbered among them that were slain for the Word of God.

10 And they cried with a loud voice, saying, How long, O Lord, holy and true, dost thou not judge and avenge our blood on them that dwell on the earth?

John is presented with a surprising picture of the martyred saints. Rather than being at peace and resting, they are crying out with a loud voice. The martyred saints have a specific question they want answered. It is a question as to when their blood will be avenged by those who dwell on the earth. Those who dwell on earth, in Revelation, are the wicked, the unrepentant, the unconverted. The saints in heaven want to know "how long" before justice is done. That is a question that every human suffering heart has asked. The Psalmist asked it many times (Ps. 94:1–7, 29). The saints in heaven want to know about their own blood avenger.

The idea of an avenger of blood was well known in Jewish culture, and in the Christian community. An avenger of blood was legally responsible for carrying out vengeance when a family member had been unlawfully injured, killed, or murdered. Normally, the avenger of blood was the nearest male relative. Justice was to be sought by killing the individual responsible for the death of the relative.

"The revenger of blood himself shall slay the murderer: when he meeteth him, he shall slay him" (Num. 35:19).

A person might flee for safety to a city of refuge (Num. 35:16, 17), but, upon examination, if found guilty, the guilty had to face the proper punishment. "But if any man hate his neighbour, and lie in wait for him, and rise up against him, and smite him mortally that he die, and fleeth into one of these cities: Then the elders of his city shall send and fetch him thence, and deliver him into the hand of the avenger of blood, that he may die" (Deut. 19:11–12).

Gideon became the avenger of blood for his brothers who had been murdered on Mount Tabor by the Midianite kings Zebah, and Zalmunna (Jdgs. 8:18–21). Joab avenged the blood of his brother Asahel (2 Sam. 3:27–30). The men of Gibeon avenged the deaths of their countrymen at the hands of Saul by executing seven of the King's sons (2 Sam. 21:1–9).

The avenger of blood concept also figures into the account of King Amaziah, who put to death the officials who had assassinated his father (2 Kgs. 14:5–6). The story of the Tekoite woman involved a plea for King David to stop the actions of the avenger of blood (2 Sam. 14:8–11).

In the New Testament, the apostle Paul instructed the church in Rome not to take vengeance on others. "Recompense to no man evil for evil. Provide things honest in the sight of all men. If it be possible, as much as lieth in you, live peaceably with all men. Dearly beloved, avenge not yourselves, but rather give place unto wrath: for it is written, Vengeance is mine; I will repay, saith the Lord" (Rom. 12:17–19).

Care must be taken not to go too far with the idea of loving ones enemies, and not taking vengeance, for then the whole notion of judging righteously, along with hell, is dismissed. There are local churches that hold no one accountable. Righteousness is perverted.

People can forget that the desire for righteous revenge is rooted in the concept of justice. Therefore, in heaven, John hears the martyred saints plead for their blood to be avenged (*ekdikeō*; to vindicate, retaliate, punish). Graciously does the Lord allow such questions to be asked, even in heaven.

11 **And white robes were given unto every one of them; and it was said unto them, that they should rest yet for a little season, until their fellow servants also and their brethren, that should be killed as they *were*, should be fulfilled.**

While the martyred saints waited and clamored for justice, they were given white robes to wear, and told to rest until their brothers and sisters in Christ could also be killed, according to divine design. John might have been surprised at the plea for a blood avenger, and equally surprised at the response given to them. Who provided the response is not stated. What is said, is that there would be more martyred saints by divine design. It has been written on the scroll that a certain number of Christians are to be killed for Christ, and the blood bath will continue until that number is fulfilled. Heaven is not the final resting place, but it is a step closer to the final resurrection, and then the new heaven and new earth.

Keeping that concept in mind, every believer must be prepared to wear the martyrs crown, called the crown of life. "Fear none of those things which thou shalt suffer: behold, the devil shall cast some of you into prison, that ye may be tried; and ye shall have tribulation ten days: be thou faithful unto death, and I will give thee a crown of life" (Rev. 2:10).

The Sixth Seal: Cosmic Disturbances

Scene One: Great Day of His Wrath

12 And I beheld when he had opened the sixth seal, and, lo, there was a great earthquake; and the sun became black as sackcloth of hair, and the moon became as blood;

Because the martyr saints asked how long before their blood was to be avenged, John saw the answer to that inquiry, though not in a sequential order, for this First Scene of the Sixth Seal speaks of The Final Judgment of the Wicked accompanied by cataclysmic events.

13 And the stars of heaven fell unto the earth, even as a fig tree casteth her untimely figs, when she is shaken of a
mighty wind. 14 And the heaven departed as a scroll when
it is rolled together; and every mountain and island were
moved out of their places. 15 And the kings of the earth,

and the great men, and the rich men, and the chief captains, and the mighty men, and every bondman, and every free man, hid themselves in the dens and in the rocks of the mountains; [16] And said to the mountains and rocks, Fall on us, and hide us from the face of him that sitteth on the throne, and from the wrath of the Lamb: [17] For the great day of his wrath is come; and who shall be able to stand?

The words of Revelation 6:12–17 form the language of the Last Judgment on the great day of God's wrath. Notice that His wrath "is come." Elsewhere, John wrote, "Little children, it is the last time: and as ye have heard that antichrist shall come, even now are there many antichrists; whereby we know that it is the last time" (1 John 2:18). For those who need signs that we are in the last time, there is plenty of evidence.

There are wars and rumors of wars; nations rise against nations. Since 1945 and the end of World War II, there have been well over 200 armed conflicts, as individuals go forth to conquer others.

There are earthquakes in various places creating tsunamis, and causing mountains to fall. In 2020, between January 1 and May 31, there were 4,863 earthquakes all over the world with a magnitude of over 4.0. Five hundred and sixty-eight other earthquakes registered more than 5.0 in magnitude. Forty-three more registered more than 6.0 in magnitude. Three were greater than 7.0. The earth does shake.

There are famines and plagues. Despite the abundance of knowledge on how to grow food, much of the world remains in hunger. A locust plague of Biblical proportion, captured on video, swarmed the Middle East and Africa decimating the crops in Ethiopia, Kenya, and elsewhere. Desert locusts can travel up to 95 miles per day, and devour as much food as 35,000 people can eat, according to a United Nations report.

There is the persecution of Christians. In the midst of the 2020 coronavirus pandemic in America—a nation who cherishes herself on protecting personal freedom and liberty, or at least once did—churches and other places of religious worship were specifically targeted to be closed, while abortion clinics, liquor stores, casinos, and businesses that sell cannabis were deemed "essential" by state governments and allowed to remain open to the public.

Many professing Christians fell away from the faith even before the Beast of government issued a formal prohibition against believers meeting. The faithful obeyed God rather than man, and found ways to forsake not the assembly.

There are many false teachers, messiahs, prophets, and apostles. Some teach a secret silent coming of Christ. Jesus said, "And then if any man shall say to you, Lo, here is Christ; or, lo, he is there; believe him not" (Mark 13:21). The Church in Ephesus was commended for testing those who said they were apostles, but were not.

There is the rise of lawlessness resulting in love growing cold in the hearts of many, to the point that babies are butchered, their body parts are sold for money, and rioters smash, destroy, and steal what others have. In nations great and small throughout the world, lawlessness persists, encouraged by militant activist groups, such as Antifa, that cover their evil under the banner of virtue. Anarchism—which is lawlessness—is inspired by Satan and his demons.

There is the preaching of the gospel to all nations. While there is much sin in the world, and though the day of God's wrath is come, there is mercy yet as the gospel is being preached in all the world to all the nations. Jesus said it would. "And this gospel of the kingdom shall be preached in all the world for a witness unto all nations; and then shall the end come" (Matt. 24:14). Many Christians have been conditioned to look for an Antichrist, and signs of the time. Most have not been taught to look for the gospel to be preached to all nations, and so lose hope and faith. There is a sense of doom and gloom. Christians admit to being afraid after reading Revelation, and so miss out on the seven blessings associated with the narrative, and the main point—the triumph of the Church.

The gospel must be preached and embraced, for no one, in and of themselves, can stand God's wrath. "O LORD, I have heard thy speech, and was afraid: O LORD, revive thy work in the midst of the years, in the midst of the years make known; in wrath remember mercy" (Hab. 3:2).

Revelation Chapter 7

Sixth Seal: Scene Two: A Reason for Delay of the Final Judgment

**1 And after these things I saw four angels standing on
the four corners of the earth, holding the four winds of
the earth, that the wind should not blow on the earth, nor
on the sea, nor on any tree. 2 And I saw another angel as-
cending from the east, having the seal of the living God:
and he cried with a loud voice to the four angels, to whom
it was given to hurt the earth and the sea,**

The Sealing of the Saints in Their Foreheads

**3 Saying, Hurt not the earth, neither the sea, nor the
trees, till we have sealed the servants of our God in their
foreheads.**

The sealing of the saints of God in their foreheads anticipate the counterfeit work of the Dragon in Revelation 13:16 who causes people to "receive a mark in their right hand, or in their foreheads." The followers of Christ receive His seal on their forehead, and the followers of the Devil receive his seal on their foreheads, *and* in their right hand. The Devil knows how to make individuals serve him with all their strength, reflected in the power associated with the right hand, and with all their hearts, represented by the seal in the forehead. Here is a mark to whom one belongs.

In the ancient world, a slave might be compelled to receive a mark so they could not deny to whom they belonged. Romans did not brand all slaves, but they might brand a recalcitrant slave, or a runaway slave, to mark him as a fugitive. The branding was a symbol that you belonged to someone. Spiritually, the symbol is the same. We are either sealed by our God, or we are sealed by the Devil. Jesus said to some Pharisees, "Ye are of your father the devil, and the lusts of your father ye will do. He was a murderer from the beginning, and abode not in the truth, because there is no truth in him. When he speaketh a lie, he speaketh of his own: for he is a liar, and the father of it" (John 8:44).

One of the visible symbolic seals the Church employs is baptism. Baptism is a sign of being born again. We are buried with Christ in the likeness of His death, and raised again in the likeness of His resurrection to walk in the newness of life. The act of baptism is a way of telling others to whom we belong. While baptism is not essential to receive forgiveness, it is imperative for obedience to the known will of the Lord who would have His disciples be baptized.

The visible seal of baptism the Church employs is to show to whom Christians belong. Baptism is a manifestation of the sealing by the Spirit. Paul explains. "In whom ye also trusted, after that ye heard the word of truth, the gospel of your salvation: in whom also after that ye believed, ye were sealed with that Holy Spirit of promise" (Eph. 1:13). At the moment of salvation, the Holy Spirit puts a divine seal on every believer. The word, seal, in the Greek, is *sphragizō* [sfrag-id-zo], and means to stamp (with a signet or private mark) for security or preservation (literally or figuratively); by implication, to keep secret to attest).

The sealing of God is a source of strength in times of tribulation. The heart can be encouraged and sing a song of praise.

> Blessed assurance, Jesus is mine!
> Oh, what a foretaste of glory divine!
> Heir of salvation, purchase of God,
> Born of His Spirit, washed in His blood.
>
> This is my story, this is my song,
> Praising my Savior all the day long;
> This is my story, this is my song,
> Praising my Savior all the day long.[1]

The sealing of God is acquired by faith. To be among those sealed by God, faith is needed in God's revelation concerning the way of salvation through faith in His Son, Jesus Christ. E. M. Bounds noted, "God's revelation does not need the light of human genius, the polish and strength of human culture, the brilliancy of human thought, the force of human brains to adorn or enforce it; but it does demand the simplicity, the docility, humility, and faith of a child's heart."

4 And I heard the number of them which were sealed:
***and there were* sealed an hundred *and* forty *and* four thou-**
sand of all the tribes of the children of Israel. 5 Of the
tribe of Juda *were* sealed twelve thousand. Of the tribe of

---

[1] Francis J. Crosby.

Reuben *were* sealed twelve thousand. Of the tribe of Gad *were* sealed twelve thousand. [6] Of the tribe of Aser *were* sealed twelve thousand. Of the tribe of Nepthalim *were* sealed twelve thousand. Of the tribe of Manasses *were* sealed twelve thousand. [7] Of the tribe of Simeon *were* sealed twelve thousand. Of the tribe of Levi *were* sealed twelve thousand. Of the tribe of Issachar *were* sealed twelve thousand. [8] Of the tribe of Zabulon *were* sealed twelve thousand. Of the tribe of Joseph *were* sealed twelve thousand. Of the tribe of Benjamin *were* sealed twelve thousand.

What this scene reveals, is that there is a reason why the Final Judgment, the ultimate day of God's wrath is delayed, though the time is accompanied by many troubles. The reason for the divine delay is that God is gathering His people, sealing the elect, and marking them on their foreheads.

Representing the elect, "of all the tribes of Israel," are 12,000 souls from each of the following tribes: Judah, Reuben, Gad, Aser, Nepthalim, Manasses, Simeon, Levi, Zebulon, Joseph, Benjamin. The tribe of Dan is missing, and replaced with the half tribe of Manasseh, the firstborn of the two sone of Joseph. Manasseh was born in Egypt to Asenath the daughter of Poti-Pherah, the priest of On (Gen. 41:50–51). The inclusion of Manasseh reminds God's people that the true Israelite is the one who has the faith of Abraham, and that would include Gentiles. "Know ye therefore that they which are of faith, the same are the children of Abraham" (Gal. 3:7).

While this list of tribes is slightly different than the original twelve tribes of Israel, the message is the same. The Jews have not been totally cast away from God. Jews will continue to be brought to faith, though it must be kept in mind that not all Israel is Israel (Rom. 9:6).

TRIBES OF ISRAEL

In Genesis Tribe	Mother	*In Revelation*
• Rueben	Leah	Judah
• Simeon	Leah	Reuben
• Levi	Leah	Gad
• Judah	Leah	Aser
• Dan*	Bilhah	Nepthalim
• Naphtali	Bilhah	Manasses*
• Gad	Zilpah	Simeon
• Asher	Zilpah	Levi
• Issachar	Leah	Issachar
• Zebulun	Leah	Zebulon
• Joseph	Rachel	Joseph
• Benjamin	Rachel	Benjamin

Consider. In Revelation, the tribe of Dan is not mentioned. It is replaced with the half-tribe of Manasses.

If the holy angels are being restrained, and they are, it is because God's people still have to be sealed. The Second Scene is an enlarged message to the souls gathered under the heavenly altar as to why they need to rest for a little season and be patient. There are more saints to be sealed, including more believers appointed, by divine design, to wear the martyrs' crown. Part of the Christian message is to prepare people to face tribulation, and even death, with courage, and the hope of ultimate conquest. "Our people die well," said John Wesley about the Methodist.

While the Lord delays His coming, and the ultimate Day of Wrath and Final Judgment, let the Church learn the lessons of life, evangelize the world, and prepare for death "as it is appointed unto men once to die, but after this the judgment" (Heb. 9:27). Those who are evangelized can be comforted, and assured, they will be preserved and protected, not from tribulation, but from the damning wrath to come on all unbelievers.

Sixth Seal: Scene Three: A Glorious Celebration

9 After this I beheld, and, lo, a great multitude, which no man could number, of all nations, and kindreds, and people, and tongues, stood before the throne, and before the Lamb, clothed with white robes, and palms in their hands;

Having given an expanded explanation to the souls under the altar that more souls are to be saved, having illustrated the many souls that will be converted with the reprehensive number of 144,000 from each of the tribes of Israel, having noted the redeemed will consist of those who have the faith of Abraham, including Jews and Gentiles, attention is given to the Third Scene associated with the Sixth Seal. In this scene, John sees a great multitude. No longer are there only 144,000 souls, but a great number of people from all nations, and languages. The redeemed stand before the Lamb as a sealed people, clothed in white robes of righteousness, with palms in their hands, and a song in their hearts.

10 And cried with a loud voice, saying, Salvation to our God which sitteth upon the throne, and unto the Lamb.

The song the saints sing is simple, beautiful, and meaningful. Salvation belongs to our God. Every person who goes to heaven will only be there because salvation belongs to God. It was God the Father who planned our salvation. It was Christ who carried out the plan of the Father.

> Jesus paid it all,
>   All to Him I owe;
> Sin had left a crimson stain,
>   He washed it white as snow.[2]

11 And all the angels stood round about the throne, and *about* the elders and the four beasts, and fell before the throne on their faces, and worshipped God, 12 Saying, Amen: Blessing, and glory, and wisdom, and thanksgiving, and honour, and power, and might, *be* unto our God for ever and ever. Amen.

Joining in the worship of the Lamb before the throne are the 144,000, the great multitude which no man could number, the angels, the elders, and the Four Living Creatures. John hears precisely what they all say in unison.

Amen.
Blessing, and glory, and wisdom,
and thanksgiving, and honour, and power, and might,
be unto our God for ever and ever.
Amen.

---

[2] Elvina M. Hall.

A Heavenly Dialogue Concerning Those Who Are Rescued

13 And one of the elders answered, saying unto me, What are these which are arrayed in white robes? And whence came they?

As John watched the great multitude before the throne, and heard the praise being given to God, an Elder had a question for the apostle. He wanted to know if John understood what he was witnessing. It is one thing to read a book, see a play, or watch history unfold, it is another matter to understand what is going on. The Elder asked John, "Who are these which are clothed in white garments? Where did they come from? John, do you understand what you are witnessing?"

John was not prepared to give an answer, or even hazard a guess. Sometimes, it is good to be humble enough to acknowledge what is not known, while being diplomatic. The apostle deftly responded to the question of the Elder by deferring the answer back to him.

14 And I said unto him, Sir, thou knowest. And he said to me, These are they which came out of great tribulation, and have washed their robes, and made them white in the blood of the Lamb.

What John did not know, and was honest enough to say in his response, the Elder did know. The Elder wanted the apostle to understand the heavenly vision. There was no reason for John to see the Revelation if he was going to witness it without understanding. John would have been very disturbed, much like Nebuchadnezzar who saw a vision but could not comprehend its meaning until Daniel explained it to him. The Elder explained to John the opening of the Sixth Seal. Simply enough, the great multitude dressed in white, with a palm branch in their hands are those who came out of great tribulation.

Since these souls were dressed in white, since they were already in heaven, since they had palm branches in their hands, and since they were singing the song of praise of thanksgiving to God for their salvation, the logical conclusion is that they had *already* gone through great tribulation, of which John said he was their partner. "I, John, who also am your brother, and companion in tribulation, and in the kingdom and patience of Jesus Christ, was in the isle that is called Patmos, for the word of God, and for the testimony of Jesus Christ." (Rev. 1:9).

In addition, John had written a letter of love from the Lord to the Church in Smyrna saying, "I know thy works, and tribulation" (Rev. 2:9). The saints in Smyrna had been told they would face more tribulation (Rev. 2:9).

Certainly, the early Church faced great tribulation. Jesus was crucified, Stephen was stoned to death. Each of the apostles suffered martyrdom, with the exception of John, who was banished to the isle of Patmos.

Prior to his conversion, Paul, as Saul of Tarsus, had persecuted those of The Way. The Jewish people persecuted the Church, and so did Rome. In A.D. 41, Agrippa I cultivated favor with the Jewish leaders and so persecuted the Christians. James lost his life to the sword (Acts 12:2). He was the brother of John. Among those whom John saw in the great multitude which no man could number was his own dear brother.

In July of A.D. 64, when a colossal fire broke out in Rome and destroyed much of the city, the Emperor Nero ordered Christians to be sought out and killed. Some were torn apart by dogs, and others were burned alive as human torches. The persecution of the early church was extensive, and produced many martyrs.

But that was not the final word, for death is not the end for a Christian. There is heaven to gain. To be away from home in the body, is to be at home in the Lord. God will still be worshiped, in heaven, with others. There is a white robe of righteousness to wear.

There is nothing mysterious, or even special in this scene. What Christians endure in life is simply great tribulation. "Man is born unto trouble as the sparks fly upward" (Job 5:7). Nevertheless, great tribulation holds no victory over the saints. Therefore, let the Church join the great multitude and sing a song of praise.

My faith looks up to Thee,
  Thou Lamb of Calvary, Savior divine!
Now hear me while I pray, take all my guilt away,
  O let me from this day be wholly Thine!

May Thy rich grace impart
  Strength to my fainting heart, my zeal inspire!
As Thou hast died for me, O may my love to Thee,
  Pure warm, and changeless be, a living fire!

While life's dark maze I tread,
  And griefs around me spread, be Thou my guide;
Bid darkness turn to day, wipe sorrows tears away,
  Nor let me ever stray from Thee aside.

When ends life's transient dream,
  When deaths cold sullen stream shall o'er me roll;

Blest Savior, then in love, fear and distrust remove;
O bear me safe above, a ransomed soul![3]

When the Lamb is the Shepherd

15 Therefore are they before the throne of God, and serve him day and night in his temple: and he that sitteth on the throne shall dwell among them.

There is a Heavenly Temple which John sees. It is called "His Temple" (God's Temple). The Heavenly Temple, God's Temple, has a heavenly altar, "them that worship therein," and the Ark of His Testament. Those who worship in the Heavenly Temple are identified as the Twenty-four elders, the Four Living Creatures, the Martyred Souls under the altar, and a great multitude dressed in white robes.

16 They shall hunger no more, neither thirst any more; neither shall the sun light on them, nor any heat. 17 For the Lamb which is in the midst of the throne shall feed them, and shall lead them unto living fountains of waters: and God shall wipe away all tears from their eyes.

The Third Scene of the Sixth Seal ends with a paradox of the Lamb being the Shepherd, to lead and feed His flock to fountains of living waters. God shall come to wipe away all tears from their eyes, to give His faithful servants peace and comfort. In heaven there is no more thirst, no more scorching sun, no oppressive heat. There is the throne of God, and His presence for ever.

---

[3] Layyah Barakat.

Revelation Chapter 8

The Seventh Seal: From the Shout of Glory to the Sound of Silence

[1] **And when he had opened the seventh seal, there was silence in heaven about the space of half an hour.**

The Seventh Seal is what it says it is, silence in heaven for half an hour. A pause was appropriate, for John has been in heavenly glory. He has been given understanding of what the scenes in the vision mean. He has witnessed incredible images conveying spiritual realities associated with actual events in the life of the saints, and the souls of those in heaven. He has seen the vast multitude before the throne. He has witnessed the One on the throne, and shown the Lamb as shepherd. He has heard the promises, and best of all, he has listened to the voices of God's creation giving majestic praise. Then, suddenly, there was silence, and the silence was golden. The Psalmist said, "Be still, and know that I am God: I will be exalted among the nations, I will be exalted in the earth" (Ps. 46:10). Silence can be dramatic.

A prolonged period of silence, under certain conditions, can seem like an eternity. When a call comes that a loved one has been hurt, and is in critical condition at the hospital, waiting on an update, even for thirty minutes, can seem like a long period of time. There is intensity in the silence of waiting. The seconds drag by. In our suffering on earth, as we endure one tribulation after another, time stands still and it seems like the pain will go on forever, but the end will soon come. When tribulation ends for the Christians, it results in something glorious.

One day, when we look back on our great ordeal in life, we will see, it was only a half hour, it was only a brief period of time. James said, "For what is your life? It is even a vapor, that appeareth for a little time, and then vanisheth away" (Jas. 4:14).

While the Christian waits amidst great events swirling around life, including tribulation, holy patience is being cultivated, which is well pleasing to the Lord. The patience of the saints is commended time and again. "I know your patience" says the Lord (Rev. 2:2, 3, 19). "Here is the patience and the faith of the saints" (Rev. 13:10), writes John, "that keep the commandments of God, and the faith of Jesus" (Rev. 14:12).

"Now the God of patience and consolation grant you to be likeminded one toward another according to Christ Jesus" (Rom. 15:5).

The Third Cycle (8:2—11:19)

The Place of Suffering in the Plan of God for the Wicked Repent or Perish

2 And I saw the seven angels which stood before God; and to them were given seven trumpets.

Once more the scene moves to the Heavenly Temple, where John is witness to seven angels standing before God with seven trumpets which were given to them. Suddenly, another angel swoops into the narrative, an eighth angel.

An Eighth Angel

3 And another angel came and stood at the altar, having a golden censer; and there was given unto him much incense, that he should offer *it* with the prayers of all saints upon the golden altar which was before the throne.

The eighth angel which John saw went and stood by the heavenly altar. He carried a golden censer with much incense, which, for the second time, John is told, incense are the prayers of the saints (Rev. 5:8). Which prayers of which saints? In context, these are the prayers of the saints under the altar in the Heavenly Temple from the Fifth Seal. Specifically, the saints had asked in prayer, "How long, O Lord, holy and true, dost thou not judge and avenge our blood on them that dwell on the earth?" (Rev. 6:10). That prayer is being answered again, in part, as the sufferings of the wicked are foretold.

4 And the smoke of the incense, *which came* with the prayers of the saints, ascended up before God out of the angel's hand.

When Christians suffer, it is easy for the heart to wonder if the Lord cares. Are prayers really being heard? The answer is that the prayers of the saints do ascend up before God. More importantly, the prayers of the saints are not only heard, they are answered, though not always in the expected way. But, sometimes they are answered as asked. The martyred saints whose souls John saw under the altar, will be pleased to know they will be avenged. The judgment on the wicked takes place with the shaking of nature itself.

[5] **And the angel took the censer, and filled it with fire of the altar, and cast *it* into the earth: and there were voices, and thunderings, and lightnings, and an earthquake.**

It is a frightening scene which unfolds before John. The sound of voices, the roar of thunder, the flashes of lightening, and the shaking of the earth can be terrifying. But then, it is meant to be.

One of the thoughts of the righteous, is that they suffer more than the wicked. The Psalmist believed this, and confessed that he was envious when he saw the prosperity of the wicked (Ps. 73:3). The Psalmist thought the wicked were better off than the righteous until he went into the sanctuary of God, and came to understand their end (Ps. 73:17). The Psalmist came to understand the desolate and dreadful judgment on the wicked. "For, lo, they that are far from thee shall perish: thou hast destroyed all them that go a whoring from thee. But it is good for me to draw near to God: I have put my trust in the Lord God, that I may declare all thy works" (Ps. 73:27–28).

The souls under the altar were wondering why they should suffer, and their blood not be avenged. John sees the wicked will suffer a fate far worse than martyrdom. Their judgment will be more severe, and last longer than any pain and suffering of the righteous. "For our light affliction, which is but for a moment, worketh for us a far more exceeding and eternal weight of glory" (2 Cor. 4:17).

6 And the seven angels which had the seven trumpets
prepared themselves to sound.

The First Trumpet

7 The first angel sounded, and there followed hail and
fire mingled with blood, and they were cast upon the
earth: and the third part of trees was burnt up, and all
green grass was burnt up.

The Second Trumpet

8 And the second angel sounded, and as it were a great
mountain burning with fire was cast into the sea: and the
third part of the sea became blood; 9 And the third part of
the creatures which were in the sea, and had life, died; and
the third part of the ships were destroyed.

The Third Trumpet

10 And the third angel sounded, and there fell a great
star from heaven, burning as it were a lamp, and it fell upon the third part of the rivers, and upon the fountains of
waters; 11 And the name of the star is called Wormwood:
and the third part of the waters became wormwood; and
many men died of the waters, because they were made bitter.

The Fourth Trumpet

[12] And the fourth angel sounded, and the third part of the sun was smitten, and the third part of the moon, and the third part of the stars; so as the third part of them was darkened, and the day shone not for a third part of it, and the night likewise. [13] And I beheld, and heard an angel flying through the midst of heaven, saying with a loud voice, Woe, woe, woe, to the inhabiters of the earth by reason of the other voices of the trumpet of the three angels, which are yet to sound!

The overwhelming force of this scene is to convey the truth that God brings judgment upon the wicked in real time in history. The justice of God is mingled with grace, but the heavy hammer of divine justice does come down on the ungodly in a variety of ways. The wicked experience hail storms, and devastating fires that are almost beyond control. Trees burn up, along with green grass. There are bloody deaths that occur. The earth shakes. Mountains explode, and the debris falls into the sea. People who live in the vicinity flee for their lives; not all escape. In a variety of ways water is polluted. The wicked drink it and are poisoned. Many die. An angel flying in heaven cries out, "Woe! Woe! Woe! to the inhabiters of the earth!" The wicked are not getting away with anything for "The arc of the moral universe is long, but it bends toward justice" (Theodore Parker, 1871). There is judgment for the wicked, and it is serious.

While the Church, including the martyred saints, should not rejoice in the suffering of the wicked, there should always be a desire to see justice in time, or in eternity. When there is justice in history, there is the opportunity to repent, to change, to be fundamentally and forever different. The desire for the martyred saints need not be viewed exclusively in the context of *lex talionis*, or the law of retaliation, whereby punishment is meted out in the form of an eye for an eye, and a tooth for a tooth. The judgment of God is design to elicit mercy from the Lord, based on gospel repentance.

The appropriate response to every school shooting, every riot, every racial murder, every Antifade uprising, every war, every pandemic, every plague, and every case of governmental corruption, is prayer, repentance, restitution, and return to the Lord. The God of nature, the God of creation, is the God of the new creation. He can give individuals a new heart. Call upon the Lord, in terror if that is the only way He can bring you to repentance, or in gratitude, that He has called you to follow the Lamb, and has spared you in the day of His wrath on the ungodly.

When the suffering in life can be traced to heaven, the objective is to bring individuals to repentance, while administering justice on the wicked.

Revelation Chapter 9

The Fifth Trumpet

1 And the fifth angel sounded, and I saw a star fall from heaven unto the earth: and to him was given the key of the bottomless pit.

The star which fell from heaven is a person, for it is said that, "to *him* was given the key of the bottomless pit." In Scripture, the key is the symbol of power, control, and authority.

Immediate interest is given to the star that fell from heaven. Can the fallen star be identified? Perhaps he can be identified, for there are very few individuals in the Bible who are said to have a key, literal or symbolic.

A brief review of Scripture reveals that the prophet Isaiah said the Messiah would be given, "the key of the house of David" (Isa. 22:22; Rev. 3:7).

Jesus said to Peter, "And I will give unto thee the keys of the kingdom of heaven: and whatsoever thou shalt bind on earth shall be bound in heaven: and whatsoever thou shalt loose on earth shall be loosed in heaven" (Matt. 16:19).

In Revelation 1:18, the resurrected Christ says that He has "the keys of hell and of death."

The Holder of Keys	What the Key Unlocked	Scripture
Servants of Eglon	Palace Parlor	Jdg. 3:25
The Messiah	House of David	Isa. 22:22
Jesus	Hell and Death	Rev. 1:18
Jesus	Key of David	Rev. 3:7
Peter, the Apostle	Key of the Kingdom of Heaven	Matt. 16:19
Lawyers	Knowledge	Luke 11:52
The Star	Bottomless Pit	Rev. 9:1
Angel	Bottomless Pit	Rev. 20:1

In Revelation 9:1 a star which has fallen (Gk. *piptō*, to fall [literally or figuratively]) is given the key to the bottomless pit. In Job 38:7, angels are referred to as "the morning stars." They once sang together, and all the sons of God shouted for joy.

With this information in mind, it is worthy of notice that the identity of an angel is given in Revelation 9:11. His name in the Hebrew tongue is Abaddon, a destroying angel, but in the Greek tongue his name is Apollyon, a destroyer (i.e. Satan).

2 **And he opened the bottomless pit; and there arose a smoke out of the pit, as the smoke of a great furnace; and the sun and the air were darkened by reason of the smoke of the pit.**

The Devils Army from the Bottomless Pit

The First Woe

3 **And there came out of the smoke locusts upon the earth: and unto them was given power, as the scorpions of the earth have power.**

The power of the scorpion is in the tail to sting, and cause either incredible pain, or death to its victim. When He chooses, God can use every evil power in the world to bring pain, suffering, and death to people. Centuries before the vision of the Revelation, the Lord had warned the ungodly, and the wicked, He would punish them with scorpions (Deut. 8:15; 1 Kgs. 12:11, 14; 2 Chron. 10:11, 14; Ezek. 2:6).

The Sovereign Over Satanic Forces

4 And it was commanded them that they should not hurt the grass of the earth, neither any green thing, neither any tree; but only those men which have not the seal of God in their foreheads.

Someone sovereignly commanded the army from hell not to harm the grass or any green thing, or tree. The grass and green things had already been harmed by the first angel with the first trumpet (Rev. 8:7).

The One who sovereignly restrains evil is Jesus who said, "All power is given unto me in heaven and in earth" (Matt. 28:18).

In Revelation, the terrible powers unleashed in the world could only hurt the wicked, who are identified by not having the seal of God in their foreheads. Let the Church hear what the Spirit has to say.

The powers from hell cannot hurt those who have been sealed by God. Oh, what a blessed truth that is, and how greatly comforting such a message will always be to God's people. Let the saints remember the promise of Jesus. "Behold, I give unto you power to tread on serpents and scorpions, and over all the power of the enemy: and nothing shall by any means hurt you. Notwithstanding in this rejoice not, that the spirits are subject unto you; but rather rejoice, because your names are written in heaven" (Luke 10:19–20).

[5] And to them it was given that they should not kill them, but that they should be tormented five months: and their torment *was* as the torment of a scorpion, when he striketh a man. [6] And in those days shall men seek death, and shall not find it; and shall desire to die, and death shall flee from them.

Despite the painful severity and torment of the scorpions from the bottomless pit, in His sovereign judgment of the wicked, God remembered to have mercy. The torment lasted for five months, which is a long time, but not as long as God could have ordained the pain and suffering to continue.

As always, the objective of suffering is not simply to punish the wicked, but to elicit repentance. Sometimes, in pain and suffering God speaks, and people listen. C. S. Lewis noted in his *The Problem of Pain*, "Pain insists upon being attended to. God whispers to us in our pleasures, speaks in our conscience, but shouts in our pain: it is His megaphone to rouse a deaf world."

In the pain which John saw being inflicted, the agony was so bad that individuals sought to die, but could not. They desired to end their pain and suffering, and life itself, but could not.

There is a quality to life as well as a quantity of days, and if the quality of life is gone, if all that a person experiences day in and day out is like the sting of a scorpion, the soul begs to die. Unless God permits, that person cannot die, no matter what human laws of euthanasia are passed. Our days are ordained by God. There is, "A time to be born, and a time to die; a time to plant, and a time to pluck up that which is planted" (Eccl. 3:2).

God has appointed the day of our birth, and the hour of our death. No one can die apart from God's permission. This truth is comforting to the righteous, and a curse to the ungodly under the wrath of the Almighty.

7 And the shapes of the locusts *were* like unto horses
prepared unto battle; and on their heads *were* as it were
crowns like gold, and their faces *were* as the faces of men. 8
And they had hair as the hair of women, and their teeth
were as *the teeth* of lions. 9 And they had breastplates, as it
were breastplates of iron; and the sound of their wings *was*
as the sound of chariots of many horses running to battle.
10 And they had tails like unto scorpions, and there were
stings in their tails: and their power *was* to hurt men five
months.

It is interesting that five months is about the life span of a locust in real life. Moreover, there is a contrast that should be noticed between the half hour of suffering of the righteous, and the five months of the wicked.

The Angel of the Pit

11 And they had a king over them, *which is* the angel of
the bottomless pit, whose name in the Hebrew tongue *is*
Abaddon, but in the Greek tongue hath *his* name Apol-
lyon. 12 One woe is past; *and,* behold, there come two woes
more hereafter.

In his vision, John is able to describe the hideous description of the locusts, and identify their leader. He is called Abaddon, in the Hebrew language, but, Apollyon in the Greek. He is the Angel of the Pit.

In the First Woe depicting the Locust from Hell, the picture is that of power, strength, terror, and horror. Because the image is symbolic, John uses the word "like" (Gk. *homoios*, similar [in appearance or character]) in verse 7, 10 and "as" (Gk. *hós*, adverb of comparison; which how, i.e. in what manner) in verses 8, and 9.

The Sixth Trumpet: Scene One: Four Angels at the Euphrates River and the Army of God: The Second Woe

13 And the sixth angel sounded, and I heard a voice from the four horns of the golden altar which is before God, 14 Saying to the sixth angel which had the trumpet, Loose the four angels which are bound in the great river Euphrates.

In contrast to the four angels who stood on the four corners of the earth, and held back the four winds of the earth to gather the elect (Rev. 7:1), these four angels are turned loose, not to gather, but to destroy.

The first four angels had a ministry that was universal in scope. Again, in contrast, these four angels are limited to the Euphrates River, which begins in Turkey, and ends in the Persian Gulf. The Great River is around 1,700 miles long. It supplies water to a large part of Western Asia.

[15] **And the four angels were loosed, which were prepared for an hour, and a day, and a month, and a year, for to slay the third part of men.**

To either flood, pollute, dam, or dry up the Euphrates River would cause many to perish. Something terrible like that was going to happen. For one year, one month, one day, and one hour, the four angels, bound in the Great River Euphrates, were turned loose to kill one third part of men. This judgment falls on some in the world in history, not on all, at the end of time.

200 Million Horsemen Ready for Battle

[16] **And the number of the army of the horsemen *were* two hundred thousand thousand: and I heard the number of them.**

In the year 2020, there are about 59 million horses in the world, which falls short of the number needed to satisfy what John *heard* in the vision in Revelation, an army of horsemen about 200 million.

The large number John heard is even more fantastic when it is realized that, at its peak, in the third century A.D., the Roman Empire only had a population of about 60–70 million. What this number would have conveyed to the Church, in particular, is that the army of God was several times larger than the whole Roman Empire, and that would have encouraged the hearts of the saints.

Jesus hinted at the large army of God when He said He could ask for twelve legions of angels to deliver Him from the Cross, and the Father would have given them to Him.

He could have called ten thousand angels
To destroy the world and set Him free
He could have called ten thousand angels
But He died alone, for you and me.

They bound the hands of Jesus
In the garden where He prayed.
They led Him thru the streets in shame.
They spat upon the Savior
So pure and free from sin
They said, "crucify Him": He's to blame

Upon His precious head
They placed a crown of thorns
They laughed and said, "Behold the king"
They struck Him and they cursed Him
And mocked His holy name.
All alone He suffered everything

When they nailed Him to the cross,
His mother stood nearby,
He said, "Woman, behold thy son!"

He cried, "I thirst for water,"
But they gave Him none to drink
Then the sinful work of man was done.

To the howling mob He yielded:
He did not for mercy cry
The cross of shame He took alone
And when He cried, "It is finished,"
He gave himself to die
Salvations wondrous plan was done.

[17] **And thus I saw the horses in the vision, and them that sat on them, having breastplates of fire, and of jacinth, and brimstone: and the heads of the horses *were* as the heads of lions; and out of their mouths issued fire and smoke and brimstone.**

The Devil's Army of locust had breastplates of iron (Rev. 9:9). In contrast, the breastplates of God's Army consist of fire, jacinth (yellow-brown), and brimstone (sulfuric rock) indicating superior strength.

The Devil's Army has locust with teeth like lions (Rev. 9:8), while God's Army has horses with the heads of lions.

The image conveyed is that God's Army is larger, stronger, and fiercer than any weapon which the Devil can form against the Christian. "No weapon that is formed against thee shall prosper; and every tongue that shall rise against thee in judgment thou shalt condemn. This is the heritage of the servants of the Lord, and their righteousness is of me, saith the Lord" (Isa. 54:17).

The Christian in complete armor, as a member of God's fortified army, shall prevail.

[18] **By these three was the third part of men killed, by the fire, and by the smoke, and by the brimstone, which issued out of their mouths.**

If individuals fear the Devil and his power, and they do, they should fear God and His power even more.

[19] **For their power is in their mouth, and in their tails: for their tails *were* like unto serpents, and had heads, and with them they do hurt.**

The locust in the Devils army had power in their tails like a scorpion (Rev. 9:10). The horses in the Lord's Army also had power in their tails, but it was like that of a serpent. Again, the instruments of pain and suffering in the Lord's Army is greater than anything in the Devils Army.

[20] **And the rest of the men which were not killed by these plagues yet repented not of the works of their hands, that they should not worship devils, and idols of gold, and silver, and brass, and stone, and of wood: which neither can see, nor hear, nor walk: [21] Neither repented they of their murders, nor of their sorceries, nor of their fornication, nor of their thefts.**

Despite the severity of God's judgment in history, individuals do not repent of murder, their involvement with the occult, and with drugs, sexual immorality, or their stealing. Ravi Zacharias said, "Sin will take you farther than you want to go, keep you longer than you want to stay, and cost you more than you want to pay."

It is one of the saddest truths in life, and it is an undeniable truth, that there are individuals so hard, they will not repent, no matter what is said or done to them. "Neither repented they."

The person with a hard heart will have no love for God, no desire for His Word, or His people, and no sense of guilt or shame over wrong behavior. The temptation comes to just say, "Let them be damned." However, a final message should go out to those with a hard heart, and who are under the wrath of God. There is still hope. John Piper explains. Though God is the decisive cause of unhardening the heart, a person can take proactive steps towards receiving a new heart.

First, even the most hardened sinners can expose themselves to the preaching of the Word. "So then faith cometh by hearing, and hearing by the word of God" (Rom. 10:17).

Second, a person can bow their head and pray. God will hear the prayers of any person, including the most sinful sinner, who prays according to His will. "And this is the confidence that we have in him, that, if we ask anything according to his will, he heareth us: And if we know that he hear us, whatsoever we ask, we know that we have the petitions that we desired of him" (1 John 5:14, 15). "God, be merciful to me a sinner" (Luke 18:13) is a prayer any cold-hearted person can pray.

Third, a person with the hardest of hard hearts can read the Bible as a book. The Bible is a fascinating piece of world literature. While waiting on a friend one day, Augustine heard voices from a neighboring house chanting, "*tolle lege*," "take up and read." Augustine picked up a Bible, in idle curiosity, and read the words of Paul the apostle to the Church in Rome. "The night is far spent, the day is at hand: let us therefore cast off the works of darkness, and let us put on the armour of light. Let us walk honestly, as in the day; not in rioting and drunkenness, not in chambering and wantonness, not in strife and envying. But put ye on the Lord Jesus Christ, and make not provision for the flesh, to fulfil the lusts thereof" (Rom. 13:12–14). God came and give him a new heart, and the Lord gave to the world St. Augustine, bishop of Hippo.

Revelation Chapter 10

The Sixth Trumpet: Scene Two: Seven Thunderous Words

1 And I saw another mighty angel come down from heaven, clothed with a cloud: and a rainbow *was* upon his head, and his face *was* as it were the sun, and his feet as pillars of fire:

There are two mighty angels referenced in Revelation. There is the mighty angel of this verse, which presupposes a prior mighty angel. Then, there is a mighty angel mentioned in Revelation 18:21. An exhaustive study of Angelology is a worthwhile study of Scripture. There should be interest in every angel mentioned in the Bible.

John says he saw an angel who was mighty (Gk. *ischuros*; forcible (literally or figuratively). The angel was boisterous, powerful, strong, valiant.

One mighty angel in the Bible mentioned by name is Michael. He has the rank of archangel (Gk., literally, "chief angel") according to Jude 9. As the archangel, Michael fought against the dragon and his angels (Rev. 12:7). Then, the angel Gabriel is mentioned by name, but not as an archangel (Luke 1:19).

[2] **And he had in his hand a little book open: and he set his right foot upon the sea, and *his* left *foot* on the earth,**

This is a majestic scene John witnesses. The mighty angel has one foot upon the sea, and the other foot on the earth. Like the Great Colossus of Rhodes, one of the Seven Wonders of the Ancient World, this personage encompasses a large part of earth. In his hand was a little book, a little scroll.

[3] **And cried with a loud voice, as *when* a lion roareth: and when he had cried, seven thunders uttered their voices.**
[4] **And when the seven thunders had uttered their voices, I was about to write: and I heard a voice from heaven saying unto me, Seal up those things which the seven thunders uttered, and write them not.**

There is information which God wants people to know. There are great spiritual truths that abide forever, such as the fact that though the righteous suffer, they will be victorious. The wicked will be judged, and will suffer far greater pain then what the ungodly inflict on the saints.

There was other information that God wanted sealed up and so, the seven thunders, or seven words uttered, were sealed, and not written down.

The conclusion of the matter is this. "The secret things belong unto the LORD our God: but those things which are revealed belong unto us, and to our children for ever, that we may do all the words of this law" (Deut. 29:29).

One lesson the Church can learn from the sealing of the little book is not to seek to know what God does not want known. It is enough that heaven knows the details of time and eternity. We should remain content where the Bible is silent.

The Announcement of the Final Judgment

**5 And the angel which I saw stand upon the sea and up-
on the earth lifted up his hand to heaven, 6 And sware by
him that liveth for ever and ever, who created heaven, and
the things that therein are, and the earth, and the things
that therein are, and the sea, and the things which are
therein, that there should be time no longer: 7 But in the
days of the voice of the seventh angel, when he shall begin
to sound, the mystery of God should be finished, as he
hath declared to his servants the prophets.**

Taking and Digesting the Little Book: Third Scene

**8 And the voice which I heard from heaven spake unto
me again, and said, Go *and* take the little book which is
open in the hand of the angel which standeth upon the sea
and upon the earth. 9 And I went unto the angel, and said
unto him, Give me the little book. And he said unto me,
Take *it*, and eat it up; and it shall make thy belly bitter,
but it shall be in thy mouth sweet as honey. 10 And I took
the little book out of the angel's hand, and ate it up; and it
was in my mouth sweet as honey: and as soon as I had eat-
en it, my belly was bitter.**

The prophet Ezekiel had this same experience. He was given a little book, or scroll to eat, and digest, which he did. The document was sweet as honey when he ate it, but became bitter in his stomach. "And he said unto me, Son of man, cause thy belly to eat, and fill thy bowels with this roll that I give thee. Then did I eat it; and it was in my mouth as honey for sweetness" (Ezek. 3:3).

What this means is that the call to study, digest, and proclaim the gospel is sweet, but it also very bitter. When gospel truth is being expressed, it is sweet to the tongue. When the gospel is rejected, it is a gut-wrenching experience for the man of God with a sensitive soul. John had a sensitive soul.

John Will Prophesy Again

11 And he said unto me, Thou must prophesy again before many peoples, and nations, and tongues, and kings.

Revelation Chapter 11

The Measuring of the Temple

[1] And there was given me a reed like unto a rod: and the
angel stood, saying, Rise, and measure the temple of God,
and the altar, and them that worship therein. [2] But the
court which is without the temple leave out, and measure
it not; for it is given unto the Gentiles: and the holy city
shall they tread under foot forty *and* two months.

With the little book being eaten, John was given a measuring rod and told to measure the Temple of God, the altar, and those that worshipped in the Temple.

What Temple is being measured here?

Up to this point in Revelation, the only Temple in view is the Heavenly Temple with an altar conveying spiritual realities (Rev. 3:12; 6:9; 7:15; 8:3, 5; 9:13). Those who worship in this Heavenly Temple have always been only the redeemed who belong to Christ. With this spiritual reality in mind, the vision continues.

The picture John sets forth is the Church, the Temple of God, surrounded on all sides by enemies which shall assault them for a period of forty-two months (1,260 days or three-

and-one-half years). While that is a long time, it is not as long as the eternity which the wicked shall have to endure in hell.

That there should be ministering and suffering for some period of time, perhaps paralleling the three-and-one-half years of the life of Christ, is to be expected. Jesus said it would happen. "'These things I have spoken unto you, that in me ye might have peace. In the world ye shall have tribulation: but be of good cheer; I have overcome the world'" (John 16:33).

The Two Witnesses

3 And I will give *power* unto my two witnesses, and they shall prophesy a thousand two hundred *and* threescore days, clothed in sackcloth.

In the Law of Moses, truth was validated by two witnesses. "At the mouth of two witnesses, or three witnesses, shall he that is worthy of death be put to death; but at the mouth of one witness he shall not be put to death" (Deut. 17:6).

As the narrative unfolds, events in the life of Moses and Elijah will be brought forward. John might have remembered how Moses and Elijah came and spoke with Jesus during His own earthly ministry on the Mount of Transfiguration. Peter, James, and John were present that day to witness the event. "And, behold, there appeared unto them Moses and Elias talking with him" (Matt. 17:3). Moses represented the Law, while Elijah represented the Prophets. Together, they established the spiritual truth that all of the Law, and each of the Prophets spoke of Christ. "And he said unto them, These are the words which I spake unto you, while I was yet with you, that all things must be fulfilled, which were written in the law of Moses, and in the prophets, and in the psalms, concerning me" (Luke 24:44).

4 **These are the two olive trees, and the two candlesticks standing before the God of the earth.**

The allusion is to Zechariah 4. "And the angel that talked with me came again, and waked me, as a man that is wakened out of his sleep, And said unto me, What seest thou? And I said, I have looked, and behold a candlestick all of gold, with a bowl upon the top of it, and his seven lamps thereon, and seven pipes to the seven lamps, which are upon the top thereof: And two olive trees by it, one upon the right side of the bowl, and the other upon the left side thereof" (Zech. 4:1–3).

In Zechariah 4, the two Jewish leaders are identified as Joshua the High Priest, and Zerubbabel the governor. They had an important work to do in rebuilding the Temple in Jerusalem that had been destroyed by Nebuchadnezzar. After 70 years in Babylonian captivity, the Jews came home to a devastated city. Much work had to be done to restore the Holy City, and a place of worship. It would be done, "Not by might, nor by power, but by my Spirit, said the Lord of hosts" (Zech. 4:6).

The images of the olive trees and candlesticks were suitable symbols of God's Holy Spirit continually supplying an abundance of power to do God's work. In Revelation, the Holy Spirit empowers the two witnesses to proclaim the gospel.

The two olive trees would provide a constant supply of oil for the lampstand. Likewise, the two witnesses would have a constant supply of oil, for they are both the olive trees, *and* the candlesticks. The witnesses of God have residual inner resources for ministry.

Jesus said, "In the last day, that great day of the feast, Jesus stood and cried, saying, If any man thirst, let him come unto me, and drink. He that believeth on me, as the scripture hath said, out of his belly shall flow rivers of living water. (But this spake he of the Spirit, which they that believe on him should receive: for the Holy Ghost was not yet *given*; because that Jesus was not yet glorified.)" (John 7:37–39).

5 And if any man will hurt them, fire proceedeth out of their mouth, and devoureth their enemies: and if any man will hurt them, he must in this manner be killed.

Just as Moses and Elijah had a protection that surrounded them, so the two witnesses are supernaturally protected. Every witness of the Lord can be assured that "No weapon that is formed against thee shall prosper; and every tongue that shall rise against thee in judgment thou shalt condemn. This is the heritage of the servants of the LORD, and their righteousness is of me, saith the LORD" (Isa. 54:17). As long as God has work to do for His servants they will be divinely protected.

6 These have power to shut heaven, that it rain not in the days of their prophecy: and have power over waters to turn them to blood, and to smite the earth with all plagues, as often as they will.

The two witnesses have power to stop rain from falling. The Bible says that "Elias was a man subject to like passions as we are, and he prayed earnestly that it might not rain: and it rained not on the earth by the space of three years and six months" (Jas. 5:17).

The two witnesses have power over water to turn water into blood, and to smite the earth with plagues, as Moses did. "And Moses and Aaron did so, as the LORD commanded; and he lifted up the rod, and smote the waters that were in the river, in the sight of Pharaoh, and in the sight of his servants; and all the waters that were in the river were turned to blood" (Exod. 7:20). Moses also struck the earth with plagues, in Egypt, by the power of God who had told His servant, "For I will at this time send all my plagues upon thine heart, and upon thy servants, and upon thy people; that thou mayest know that there is none like me in all the earth" (Exod. 9:14).

Notice that the two witnesses were protected "in the days of their prophecy." That was the work God gave them to do. That is the work of the Church. "Wherefore, brethren, covet to prophesy" (1 Cor. 14:39). The Church is to speak under inspiration, and foretell, not just future events such as the Second Advent, the resurrection of the dead, the judgment to come, and the new heaven and new earth; the Church is to speak forth the truth about the ruin of man, the redemption Jesus provides, and the need to be regenerated by the Holy Spirit.

Ministry, Death, Resurrection, and Glory: War on the Saints: First Mention of the Beast

7 **And when they shall have finished their testimony, the beast that ascendeth out of the bottomless pit shall make war against them, and shall overcome them, and kill them.**

When the two witnesses finished their testimony, when the two witnesses had conveyed the message God gave them to speak, the Enemy roared in anger, and made war on the saints.

The idea of spiritual warfare is a large theme in Scripture. The Christian is told to put on the whole armor of God (Eph.

6:10–18). The believer is to endure hardships as a good solider (2 Tim. 2:3). The heart is to be garrisoned (Phil. 4:7). The saint is to remain on guard, and stand firm in the faith. He is to be courageous and strong (1 Cor. 16:13). All of this must be done, because every Christian is part of the angelic conflict. There is war on the saints. It is orchestrated by the Beast from the Bottomless Pit. At times, the Beast shall prevail, and shall overcome Christians, and kill them. It is the will of God (Rev. 6:11).

8 And their dead bodies *shall lie* in the street of the great city, which spiritually is called Sodom and Egypt, where also our Lord was crucified.

The Great City is the City of Jerusalem. Initially, Jerusalem is called, in Revelation, a Holy City, because that is where the Temple was (Rev. 11:2). It is called the Great City, where the Lord was crucified (Rev. 11:8). It will become a Destroyed City when judged (Rev. 11:13). Judgment will fall because the Great City has become unholy, which is why she is spiritually called Sodom and Egypt, a reminder of whom God once judged severely.

Lest the hearts of God's people become too discouraged, one day, the Great City will become a New City, the New Jerusalem, coming down from God out of heaven (Rev. 21:2). Therefore, Church, keep your eye on the future. The best is yet to come.

For now, the best that can be said, scripturally, is that the Great City, spiritually called Sodom and Egypt because it has become an Unholy City, is an Important City. Jerusalem is important to the world politically, militarily, culturally, geographically, religiously, and symbolically. However, care must be taken to stay within Biblical imagery concerning Jerusalem. In relation to God's covenantal work and relationship with His people, the mind is drawn to the Heavenly Temple, where our citizenship is, and the New Jerusalem which will be found in the coming New Heaven and New Earth wherein righteousness dwells.

> For ye are not come unto the mount that might be touched, and that burned with fire, nor unto blackness, and darkness, and tempest, And the sound of a trumpet, and the voice of words; which voice they that heard intreated that the word should not be spoken to them any more: (For they could not endure that which was commanded, And if so much as a beast touch the mountain, it shall be stoned, or thrust through with a dart: And so terrible was the sight, that Moses said, I exceedingly fear and quake:) But ye are come unto mount Sion, and unto the city of the living God, the heavenly Jerusalem, and to an innumerable company of angels, To the general assembly and church of the firstborn, which are written in heaven, and to God the Judge of all, and to the spirits of just men made perfect, And to Jesus the mediator of the new covenant, and to the blood of sprinkling, that speaketh better things than that of Abel. See that ye refuse not him that speaketh. For if they escaped not who refused him that spake on earth, much more shall not we escape, if we turn away from him that speaketh from heaven (Heb. 12:18–25).

9 **And they of the people and kindreds and tongues and nations shall see their dead bodies three days and an half, and shall not suffer their dead bodies to be put in graves.**

It is a compelling scene set forth. The two protected witnesses, who had been filled with the Spirit of God, who had prophesied and performed signs and wonders, were dead. Suddenly, their testimony came to an end. They became vernable, and the Beast, mentioned for the first time, killed them. Their dead bodies had to lie in the street of the Holy City, Jerusalem, where the Lord was crucified, for three and a half days. No one was allowed to put their bodies into a grave.

10 And they that dwell upon the earth shall rejoice over them, and make merry, and shall send gifts one to another; because these two prophets tormented them that dwelt on the earth.

When the Beast killed the two witnesses, who simply preached the Word of God, the earth rejoiced because it thought the voices of prophecy had been silenced forever. People celebrated, and exchanged gifts, much like Christmas. In a perverted twisting of words and ideas the world accused the saints of tormenting them.

No, the two witnesses did not torment the world, but they did witness, and judge the world. To a guilty conscience the Word of God can be torture. When John the Baptist spoke against the unlawful marriage of Herod the tetrarch, the woman he married hated John for that. When the opportunity came, she demanded the head of the Baptizer on a platter. The deed was done. The head of John was put on a serving tray, and given to a dancing damsel who took it to her mother, Herodias (Matt. 13:1–11). Despite silencing the voice of John, her guilt and shame remained. Sin does not cease to be sin just because of silence.

**11 And after three days and an half the Spirit of life
from God entered into them, and they stood upon their
feet; and great fear fell upon them which saw them. 12 And
they heard a great voice from heaven saying unto them,
Come up hither. And they ascended up to heaven in a
cloud; and their enemies beheld them.**

As John considered the scene, suddenly a breath of life fell upon the two dead witnesses. They stood upon their feet, causing great fear to come upon those on earth which saw them. In a moment, the happiness of the world ended. The exchanging of gifts stopped. The merriment turned to astonishment. While the world wondered, the people heard a voice from heaven. It spoke to the two witnesses.

The words were understandable. The voice said, "Come up here!" It was a commanding voice that had to be obeyed. Without any effort of their own, the two witnesses went up to heaven in a cloud, just like the Lord Jesus. "And when he had spoken these things, while they beheld, he was taken up; and a cloud received him out of their sight" (Acts 1:9). This was no secret departure from earth in the middle of the night. This ascension of the two witnesses occurred in the middle of the fourth day after their execution.

**13 And the same hour was there a great earthquake, and
the tenth part of the city fell, and in the earthquake were
slain of men seven thousand: and the remnant were af-
frighted, and gave glory to the God of heaven.**

The hour of victory, the hour of glory, the hour of ascension for the saints became the hour of judgment on the world. Within the same hour of the departure of the two witnesses, John saw the earth begin to shake. A tenth part of the Holy

City of Jerusalem was destroyed. Seven thousand people died. The rest of the inhabitants in the city were terrified, and, in their fear, began to give glory to the God of heaven.

Is this an authentic conversion of seven thousand souls? Only God knows. It is possible for signs and wonders, mixed with pain and suffering, death and destruction, and acts of God in nature, to lead people to repentance. It does not happen all the time, or to everyone, for the heart of a person can be exceedingly hard and stubborn, but gospel repentance can, and does happen. Certainly, to know the terror of the Lord is an incentive for evangelism. "Knowing therefore the terror of the Lord, we persuade men; but we are made manifest unto God; and I trust also are made manifest in your consciences" (2 Cor 5:11). It is good to read that the people "gave glory to the God of heaven." *Soli Deo Gloria!*

14 The second woe is past; *and*, behold, the third woe cometh quickly.

The Second Woe is that God sends His messengers which are effective in communicating the gospel, only to be assaulted, even unto death. Despite rejection, the victory belongs to the Lord who shall raise His people up, glorify them, and dwell in their midst forever and ever.

The Seventh Trumpet: The Kingdoms of this World Belong to King Jesus: The Third Woe

15 And the seventh angel sounded; and there were great voices in heaven, saying, The kingdoms of this world are become *the kingdoms* of our Lord, and of his Christ; and he shall reign for ever and ever.

The words of this passage must not be relegated to the future, for Christ has already begun to rule and reign. Certainly, Christ sovereignly reigns over the Churches, as the Letters of Love that were written to each one indicates. But there is more. The risen Christ is even now the ascended "King of kings, and Lord of lords" (Rev. 19:16). King Jesus has sat down at the right hand of God (Heb. 10:12). When a king sits on His throne, the court is in session, judgments are made, decisions are decreed, and the sovereign commands His subject.

If Christ does not currently wield the absolute power in heaven and earth that has been given to Him, then who is in control?

The practical problems arise when people begin to think, teach, and talk about the royal reign of Christ in terms of their own imagination, hopes, dreams, and desires, rather in terms of Biblical revelation. Because Christ is to reign "for ever and ever," then He must be reigning now. If Christ is reigning now, then the nature of His reign is far different from what certain theological constructs believe.

To encourage the hearts of the saints in the sovereign reign of Jesus, John is told that the kingdoms of this world belong to our Lord, today. Tomorrow they will belong to the Lord, and all of the tomorrows as well, for "He shall reign for ever and ever." Kings and kingdoms will all pass away, but not King Jesus, or His kingdom.

The kingdom reign of Christ is a current reality, for it is in Him that we "live and move and have our being" (Acts 17:29). "Now unto the King eternal, immortal, invisible, the only wise God, be honour and glory for ever and ever. Amen" (1 Tim. 1:17).

16 And the four and twenty elders, which sat before God on their seats, fell upon their faces, and worshipped God,

O worship the King all-glorious above,
O gratefully sing his power and his love:
Our shield and defender, the Ancient of Days,
Pavilioned in splendor and girded with praise.

17 Saying, We give thee thanks, O Lord God Almighty, which art, and wast, and art to come; because thou hast taken to thee thy great power, and hast reigned.

Those who know the truth of the eternal reign of Christ are able to worship the King.

All hail King Jesus,
All hail Emmanuel.
King of Kings,
Lord of Lords,
Bright Morning Star.

And throughout eternity,
I'll sing Your praises,
And I'll reign with You throughout eternity.

18 And the nations were angry, and thy wrath is come, and the time of the dead, that they should be judged, and that thou shouldest give reward unto thy servants the prophets, and to the saints, and them that fear thy name, small and great; and shouldest destroy them which destroy the earth.

It is because Jesus sovereignly rules and reigns that the nations rage against Him. Petty rulers and people in the nations on earth puff themselves up and say, "We will not have this Man to rule over us!" Nevertheless, our God reigns which is why He is able to keep us from falling, and to present His followers "faultless before the presence of his glory with exceeding joy, To the only wise God our Saviour, be glory and majesty, dominion and power, both now and ever. Amen" (Jude 24–25).

> O tell of his might and sing of his grace,
> whose robe is the light, whose canopy space.
> His chariots of wrath the deep thunderclouds form,
> and dark is his path on the wings of the storm.[1]

[19] **And the temple of God was opened in heaven, and there was seen in his temple the ark of his testament: and there were lightnings, and voices, and thunderings, and an earthquake, and great hail.**

The vision of an open Temple of God displaying the Ark of the Covenant would have been a thrilling view for John, because all through Jewish history the Ark of the Covenant was not on display. During the wilderness it was covered, and in the Temple it was inside the Holy of Holies where only the High Priest could go, and then, only once a year on the Day of Atonement.

The shape and size of the Ark was established by Moses in Exodus 25:10–22. A box made of acacia wood, overlaid with gold inside and out, was to be constructed, two cubits and a half in length, by a cubit and a half in breadth, and a cubit and a half in height (45 inches in length x 27 inches in breadth x

---

[1] Robert Grant.

27 inches in height). Inside the box was to be placed the two tablets of stone upon which were written the Ten Commandments. On top of the Ark was to be a basin, looked down upon by two angels with outstretched wings that touched.

Today, there are some devout religious people who sincerely believe the Ark of the Covenant was taken from Jerusalem almost 3,000 years ago, during the reign of King Solomon, to a place called Aksum, in northern Ethiopia where it is housed and guarded by the monks of Saint Mary of Zion. The Jewish Virtual Library explains:

> A more plausible claim is that of archaeologist Leen Ritmeyer, who has conducted research on the Temple Mount and inside the Dome of the Rock. He claims to have found the spot on the Mount where the Holy of Holies was located during the First Temple period. In the precise center of that spot is a section of bedrock cut out in dimensions that may match those of the Ark as reported in Exodus. This section of the mount, inci-

dentally, is the one from which the creation of the world began, according to midrash (T. Kedoshim, 10). Based on his findings, Ritmeyer has postulated that the Ark may be buried deep inside the Temple Mount. However, it is unlikely that any excavation will ever be allowed on the Mount by the Muslim or Israeli authorities.

The Ark of the Covenant is important because it contained the Ten Commandments, the Moral Law of God, which Jesus kept. The Ark also contained the rod of Aaron that budded, a symbol of resurrection, the resurrection of Jesus. The Ark housed a jar of manna, the bread of heaven. Jesus said He was that bread. Covering the Ark was the Mercy Seat. Jesus is our Mercy Seat for in Him sin was judged.

The Third Woe is ended for the rejoicing of the righteous is woe to the wicked. While the wicked can hurt the righteous, the ungodly will not go unchallenged. They will suffer as well. The saints will be avenged. Here is a message of comfort for the Church.

The Heavenly Temple

The Heavenly Temple does Exist: Rev. 16:17

The Heavenly Temple is Referenced

- His Temple: Rev. 7:5; 11:19
- The Temple of God: Rev. 11:19
- The Temple of the Tabernacle of the Testimony: Rev. 15:5

The Heavenly Temple has Structural Support

- Faithful Christians: Rev. 3:12

The Heavenly Temple is Furnished

- A throne room: Rev. 4:2
- Bowls of Incense (prayers): Rev. 5:8; 8:4
- Altar (of Burnt Offering): Rev. 6:9
- Golder Altar (of Incense): Rev. 8:3
- Ark of His Testament (Ark of Covenant): Rev. 11:19; 15:5–8

The Heavenly Temple has a High Priest: Heb. 9:11; 23–24

The Heavenly Temple is a Place of Worship

- Twenty-four elders: Rev. 4:4
- Four Beasts (Living Creatures): Rev. 4:5
- The Martyred Saints: Rev. 6:9
- A Great Multitude dressed in white robes: Rev. 7:9
- Angels: Rev. 14:15, 17; 15:6

The Heavenly Temple is Open in Heaven: Rev. 11:19

The Heavenly Temple sends forth a Voice: Rev. 16:1

The Heavenly Temple is Transitional: Rev. 21:22

Revelation Chapter 12

The Fourth Cycle (12:1—14:5)

Scene One: A Woman Travailing in Birth

1 And there appeared a great wonder in heaven; a woman clothed with the sun, and the moon under her feet, and upon her head a crown of twelve stars:

As the vision continued, there appeared a great wonder (Gk. *sēmeion*; a sign) in heaven. The sign in heaven is a symbol of spiritual reality.

2 And she being with child cried, travailing in birth, and pained to be delivered.

Here is the picture of a glorious woman, established in the eternal state in heaven, in labor. The temptation comes to understand the woman to be Mary, and with good reason. Mary was favored among women and so she was glorious. Mary was pregnant, and she did travail in birth with the baby Jesus.

However, there is another understanding of the wonder, or sign in heaven. In a comprehensive way, the woman is better understood as a symbol for the Church because of the events set forth, in verses 1–5, and the subsequent activity in verses 6–12.

Scene Two: A Great Red Dragon

3 And there appeared another wonder in heaven; and behold a great red dragon, having seven heads and ten horns, and seven crowns upon his heads.

There appeared another wonder (Gk. *sēmeion*; a sign), a red (Gk. *purrhos*; fiery) dragon. A dragon (Gk. *drakōn*; serpent) in Scripture is a symbol of great power. Figurative, the term is used of Satan, the serpent, known for craftiness and malignity. The serpent fascinates people. He wants people to think he has horns of power, and crowns of glory in an exalted state.

4 And his tail drew the third part of the stars of heaven, and did cast them to the earth: and the dragon stood before the woman which was ready to be delivered, for to devour her child as soon as it was born.

Satanic Counterfeit and Opposition

- The woman is clothed with the sun. (Rev. 12:1)
  The dragon is fiery red. (Rev. 12:3)

- The woman is sovereign over twelve stars. (Rev. 12:1)
  The dragon draws a third part of the stars. (Rev. 12:3)

- The woman wears a crown. (Rev. 12:1)
  The dragon wears a crown. (Rev. 12:3)

- The woman delivers a man child. (Rev. 12:5)
  The dragon seeks to kill the man child. (Rev. 12:4)

- The Lamb has horns of power. (Rev. 5:6)
  The dragon has horns of power. (Rev. 12:3)

- The Man Child rules all nations. (Revelation 12:5)
  The Dragon demands worship by all. (Revelation 13:4)

- Jesus had a public ministry of three- and one-half years. (Rev. 12:1)
  The Dragon pursues Christ for three- and one-half years. (Rev. 12:15–17)

- Michael has a heavenly host ready for battle. (Rev. 12:7)
  Satan has a heavenly host ready to fight. (Rev. 12:7–9)

- God has His Prophet. (John 7:16; 8:28)
  The Dragon has his prophet. (Rev. 12:9; 13:11–12)

- Jesus is the Morning Star. (Rev. 22:16)
  Satan, is known as Lucifer (Heb. *heylel*), lit. the shining one; the morning star. (Isa. 14:12)

- God brought judgment on a wicked angel. (Rev. 12:9)
  Satan seeks to bring judgment against the righteous Church. (Rev. 12:13)

- Jesus is the Lion of the Tribe of Judah. (Rev. 5:5)
  Satan goes about as a roaring lion. (Rev. 12:17; 1 Pet. 5:8)

- Holy Trinity of Father, Son, Spirit (Rev. 1)
  Unholy Trinity of Dragon, Creature from Sea and Earth (Rev. 12:3; 13:1, 11)

- Jesus spoke what was given to Him. (John 12:49)
  The Dragon gives a message to his servant. (Rev. 13:4)

5 And she brought forth a man child, who was to rule all nations with a rod of iron: and her child was caught up unto God, and *to* his throne.

Though it is a symbol, the substance is clear. Jesus rules all nations with a rod of iron. The Messiah was commanded to, "Ask of me, and I shall give you the nations for your inheritance, and the uttermost parts of the earth for your possession" (Ps. 2:8). Jesus asked, and He was given all power in heaven and in earth so that His gospel could go into all the nations (Matt. 28:18–20).

The man child was pursued by the Fiery Dragon. Just as He was about to be overtaken, the child was caught up unto God, and to His throne. While the *baby* Jesus did not go to heaven, He was protected by God. When the baby Jesus was attacked by Herod, He was protected. When the Jews tried to kill Him, Jesus was protected. When people took up stones against the Lord, He was protected, for His appointed hour at Calvary had not yet come.

The Messiah Jesus eventually ascended unto God, and to His throne where He sits enthroned today. "Wherefore God also hath highly exalted him, and given him a name which is above every name: That at the name of Jesus every knee should bow, of things in heaven, and things in earth, and things under the earth; And that every tongue should confess that Jesus Christ is Lord, to the glory of God the Father" (Phil. 2:9–11).

6 And the woman fled into the wilderness, where she hath a place prepared of God, that they should feed her there a thousand two hundred *and* threescore days.

The conflict in heaven, became the conflict on earth, for the Church in particular. The apostle Paul wrote, "For we wrestle not against flesh and blood, but against principalities, against powers, against the rulers of the darkness of this world, against spiritual wickedness in high places" (Eph. 6:12). In the book of Job, the scene opens in the court of heaven. The patriarch is accused of serving God for selfish reasons. That is what the Dragon, the Serpent does, He accuses. He accused God of being unfair to Adam and Eve (Gen. 3:1–4). He accused Job of not sincerely loving God (Job 2:1–6). He accuses the brethren day and night (Rev. 12:10).

The brethren refer to the Church. It is the Church that is pursued by the Dragon. It is the Church the Dragon wants to destroy. It is the Church which must be protected by God. The number of days of divine protection is given here as one thousand, two hundred, and sixty days, or three-and-one-half years, reflecting the length of the ministry of Jesus who was protected until His hour had come to suffer at Calvary.

Three-and-One-Half Years

- Days: a thousand, two hundred, and threescore or sixty days—Rev. 12:6
- Months: forty two months—Rev. 11:2; 13:6
- Years: a time (1 year), times (2 years), and half a time (1/2 year)—Rev. 12:14

Scene Three: War in Heaven: Michael vs. The Dragon

7 **And there was war in heaven: Michael and his angels fought against the dragon; and the dragon fought and his angels,**

From the prophet Daniel, it is learned that Michael the archangel is a protector and defender of God's people. Here, Michael is presented in that role. The Dragon does not make war against God. The Dragon does not make war against Christ. The Dragon makes war against other angels. There is a spiritual reality that the Church does not see, though we are informed it exists. "For we wrestle not against flesh and blood, but against principalities, against powers, against the rulers of the darkness of this world, against spiritual wickedness in high places" (Eph. 6:12).

8 And prevailed not; neither was their place found any more in heaven. 9 And the great dragon was cast out, that old serpent, called the Devil, and Satan, which deceiveth the whole world: he was cast out into the earth, and his angels were cast out with him.

Time and again in Revelation, there is self-explanation, and internal interpretation. John wants readers to know that the Great Dragon is that Old Serpent, called the Devil, and called Satan. The symbolism of Scripture conveying spiritual truths must not be pressed beyond a Biblical boundary.

Satanic Names in Scripture

- The tempter—Matthew 4:3; 1 Thessalonians 3:5
- The evil one—Matthew 13:28, 39
- A murderer—John 8:44
- A liar—John 8:44
- The father of lies—John 8:44
- The god of this world—2 Corinthians 4:4
- The prince of the power of the air—Ephesians 2:2

- The adversary—1 Peter 5:8
- The great dragon—Revelation 12:9
- The ancient serpent—Revelation 12:9
- The Devil—Revelation 12:9
- The deceiver of the whole world—Revelation 12:9
- The accuser of our brethren—Revelation 12:10

As to why Satan would make war in heaven, there is a great mystery. The prophet Isaiah writes of how ambition and pride was manifested by the Enemy, and he was cast down.

> How art thou fallen from heaven, O Lucifer, son of the morning! how art thou cut down to the ground, which didst weaken the nations! For thou hast said in thine heart, I will ascend into heaven, I will exalt my throne above the stars of God: I will sit also upon the mount of the congregation, in the sides of the north. I will ascend above the heights of the clouds; I will be like the most High. Yet thou shalt be brought down to hell, to the sides of the pit (Isa. 14:12–15).

The initial, and the final defeat of Satan has never been in doubt. Whatever dark thoughts Lucifer (*heylel*; [in the sense of brightness]; the morning star) might have had, God remains sovereign, and He will not share His essential glory, honor, and power with anyone.

Victory!

10 **And I heard a loud voice saying in heaven, Now is come salvation, and strength, and the kingdom of our God, and the power of his Christ: for the accuser of our**

brethren is cast down, which accused them before our God day and night.

If there is a word to describe Christianity, it is the word victory! Jesus never gave up until He cried, "Telelestai! It is finished!" There was the victory of the cross. Revelation is the vision of victory. "Now is come salvation." Now, after the Devil has tried to destroy the woman and her seed. Now, after the Dragon and his angels had made war in heaven. Now, after the Old Serpent was cast down to earth. There is victory.

During World War II, when Winston Church, the Prime Minister of England asked rhetorically, "What is our policy?" He answered by saying, "Victory at all costs, victory in spite of all terror, victory however long and hard the road may be; for without victory, there is no survival."

11 **And they overcame him by the blood of the Lamb, and by the word of their testimony; and they loved not their lives unto the death.**

"They", refers to the brethren. The brethren, the Church overcomes the Dragon, the Devil, Satan, by the blood of the Lamb. The victory is not in the flesh, but in the blood.

> There is power, power, wonder-working power
> In the blood of the Lamb.
> There is power, power, wonder-working power
> In the precious blood of the Lamb.[1]

12 **Therefore rejoice, *ye* heavens, and ye that dwell in them. Woe to the inhabiters of the earth and of the sea!**

---

[1] Lewis E. Jones.

For the devil is come down unto you, having great wrath, because he knoweth that he hath but a short time.

There are important scenes pictured here. Losing his power and position in heaven, the Devil is cast down to earth. There is great rejoicing in heaven that the Devil is cast down. There is the command to rejoice.

Who dwells in heaven? God is in heaven, Christ is in heaven, the martyred saints are in heaven, the twenty four elders are in heaven, the four Living Creatures are in heaven, a great multitude is in heaven, and, scripturally, the Church is in heaven, for Christ "hath raised us up together, and made us sit together in heavenly places in Christ Jesus" (Eph. 2:6).

In the Revelation, the idea is conveyed that those who dwell in heaven are the believers. Those who dwell on earth are unbelievers. They are the ones to primarily know woe "for the Devil has come unto you"—you who are ungodly and unbelieving.

For the Christian, life on earth in the visible reality is full of sadness, sorrow, sickness, and suffering, there is a spiritual reality which only the eye of faith can behold. The truth about Christians is that we are already citizens of heaven. "For our conversation [Gk. *politeuma*; community, i.e. (abstractly) citizenship] is in heaven; from whence also we look for the Saviour, the Lord Jesus Christ: Who shall change our vile body, that it may be fashioned like unto his glorious body, according to the working whereby he is able even to subdue all things unto himself" (Phil. 3:20–21).

If we believe in Jesus, we are assured that we are protected, because Satan is cast down. Rejoice, Church! And again, I say, rejoice! Satan is cast down. Jesus saw it happen. "I beheld Satan as lightening fall from heaven" (Luke 10:18). John saw it happen. By faith, every Christian can "see" it happened with a twofold result. First, salvation has come, and strength. Second, the kingdom of our God has come, and the power of His Christ.

While there is rejoicing in heaven, there is woe to those who dwell on the earth, and those that inhabit the sea, and the Church is reminded that we live in a multidimensional world. There is the physical world, and there is the spiritual world. There is physical reality, and there is spiritual reality. In the prophetic quest neither one needs to be surrendered.

In the spiritual world, Satan seeks to damage, destroy, and damn as many souls as possible. Why? Part of this answer is that the Devil knows that he has but a short time. The Devil knows that God created hell for him and his angels.

The Fourth Cycle

Scene Four: Persecution of the Woman and Her Seed: The Center of Revelation

[13] And when the dragon saw that he was cast unto the earth, he persecuted the woman which brought forth the man *child.* [14] And to the woman were given two wings of a great eagle, that she might fly into the wilderness, into her place, where she is nourished for a time, and times, and half a time, from the face of the serpent.

The picture John sees, is the ability of the woman, who is able to flee from the Evil One who cannot completely destroy the Church.

The Church flees to the wilderness, a dry and desolate place, where the Church shall dwell until Jesus returns the Second Time for all who believe. The Church of the Old Testament (Acts 7:38), was in a literal and spiritual wilderness for at least forty years, and so is the New Testament Church (Rev. 12:14). We are not yet in the Promised Land. Someday, we will get to that special place to which we are going.

> On Jordan's stormy banks I stand,
> And cast a wishful eye
> To Canaan's fair and happy land,
> Where my possessions lie.
>
> I am bound for the promised land,
> I am bound for the promised land;
> Oh who will come and go with me?
> I am bound for the promised land.[2]

Though the Church has to flee, though the Church is pursued to be persecuted, she will ultimately be protected and sustained. The Gates of Hell shall not prevail against her, though Satan roars, his demons roam the earth, and the Enemy restricts access to places of worship. It is only for a short period called, a time, and times, and half a time. This is the same as three-and-one-half years, or 42 months, or 1,260 days.

This is the short time Satan is said to have to hurt the woman and her seed. The spiritual reality is perceived. The Devil is very angry with the Church. He pursues the Church, but she is protected for as long as the Devil is at work. Do Christians suffer? We do, but, "our light affliction, which is but for a mo-

---

[2] Samuel Stennett.

ment, worketh for us a far more exceeding and eternal weight of glory" (2 Cor. 4:17).

15 **And the serpent cast out of his mouth water as a flood after the woman, that he might cause her to be carried away of the flood.**
16 And the earth helped the woman, and the earth opened her mouth, and swallowed up the flood which the dragon cast out of his mouth.

Because the earth has no mouth, this is a symbol, a symbol of the defense of the Church which is sovereignly controlled by God.

17 **And the dragon was wroth with the woman, and went to make war with the remnant of her seed, which keep the commandments of God, and have the testimony of Jesus Christ.**

While the Enemy cannot destroy the Church as a whole, he can hurt and kill individual members of the Church. For this reason, Satan stalks about seeking individuals whom he may devour. Therefore, Christian, "Be sober, be vigilant; because your adversary the devil, as a roaring lion, walketh about, seeking whom he may devour" (1 Pet. 5:8). Whom will the Enemy stalk? Whom will Satan seek to destroy? Satan will make war with those who keep the commandments of God. He will try to silence the testimony of anyone who confesses Jesus Christ is lord.

Here is the history of the Church in summary. There is a called-out assembly, and there is a Devil. The Evil One makes war against the saints. He wants to destroy the Church, but is unable to accomplish that objective. In his wrath, the Enemy does his best to hurt the Church. However, the Devil cannot conquer the Church. *Soli Deo Gloria!*

Revelation Chapter 13

THE FOURTH CYCLE

Scene Five: The First Beast: The Creature from the Sea

1 And I stood upon the sand of the sea, and saw a beast rise up out of the sea, having seven heads and ten horns, and upon his horns ten crowns, and upon his heads the name of blasphemy.

The sea can be a very turbulent place. People die at sea. Storms blow in from the sea. Death and destruction can come from the sea. John says that he stood upon the sand of the Mediterranean Sea when he saw a vision of a beast (Gk. *therion*; a dangerous animal) rise up out of the water. The creature was terrifying for it had seven heads and ten horns. On each horn was a crown. On each head was write name of blasphemy (Gk. *blasphemia*; vilification [especially against God]). This Beast from the Sea is a servant of the Dragon, and so, is very much like the Dragon in appearance, behavior, and objectives.

Dragon	**Beast from the Sea**
Revelation 12:3–4	**Revelation 13:1–3**
Fiery red in color	Seven heads
Seven heads	Ten horns
Ten horns	Ten crowns
Seven crowns	Name of blasphemy on each head
A tail	Body of a leopard
	Feet of a bear
	Mouth of a lion
	One of the seven heads wounded
Was worshipped	Was worshipped
Waged war on the woman and her seed	Waged war on the saints

2 **And the beast which I saw was like unto a leopard, and his feet were as *the feet* of a bear, and his mouth as the mouth of a lion: and the dragon gave him his power, and his seat, and great authority.**
3 **And I saw one of his heads as it were wounded to death; and his deadly wound was healed: and all the world wondered after the beast.**

The Beast from the Sea *seemed* to have died, but was healed. Herein is a cheap counterfeit imitation of the resurrection of Christ who really died, and rose again from the dead. The Beast was simply trying to draw the world to Himself as Jesus said He would do. "And I, if I be lifted up from the earth, will draw all men unto me" (John 12:32).

Worship of the Dragon: Worship of the Creature from the Sea

4 **And they worshipped the dragon which gave power unto the beast: and they worshipped the beast, saying, Who *is* like unto the beast? Who is able to make war with him?**

The person and power behind the Creature from the Sea was the Dragon, that Old Serpent, Satan, the Devil. So great were those who dwelt upon the earth, they could not imagine anyone, more powerful than Satan, or able to overcome him. Spiritually, this is the story of David against Goliath, or the Church against the power of the Evil One.

5 **And there was given unto him a mouth speaking great things and blasphemies; and power was given unto him to continue forty *and* two months.**

The Creature from the Sea was *given* the gift of fearless eloquence to boldly speak blasphemies. As God the Father gives gifts to His children, so the Dragon *gives* gifts to his servants.

Time in Revelation

- Tribulation in Smyrna—Ten days (Rev. 2:10)
- Silence in heaven—Half an hour (Rev. 8:1)
- Slaughter by Four angels—A year, a day, a month, an hour (Rev. 9:15)
- The Gentile Nations Forty and two months trodden down (Rev. 11:1–2)
- The Two Witnesses—Three days (Rev. 11:9)
- The Two Witnesses—A thousand two hundred and threescore days (Rev. 11:3)

- The Women—A thousand two hundred and threescore days (Rev. 12:6)
- The Woman—A time, and times, and half a time (Rev. 12: 14)
- The Beast from the Sea—Forty-and-two-months (Rev. 13:5)
- Power as kings—One hour (Rev. 17:12)
- Judgment of Babylon—One hour (Rev. 18:10, 19)
- Judgment on riches—One hour (Rev. 18:17, 19)

6 **And he opened his mouth in blasphemy against God, to blaspheme his name, and his tabernacle, and them that dwell in heaven.**

The Creature from the Sea spoke against God, the name of God, the heavenly tabernacle, or dwelling place, and all that dwell in heaven, including the Twenty-four Elders, the Four Living Creatures, the Martyred Saints, the Great Multitude clothed in white, and Michael and his angels.

7 **And it was given unto him to make war with the saints, and to overcome them: and power was given him over all kindreds, and tongues, and nations.**

One way the Dragon made war on the saints was to promote the false religion of worship of the Creature from the Sea. For forty-two months, 1,260 days, or three-and-one-half years' power was given to the Creature from the Sea over all people, and tongues, provided their names were not in the Book of Life. The power over the saints was only an apparent power, not a real power.

8 And all that dwell upon the earth shall worship him, whose names are not written in the book of life of the Lamb slain from the foundation of the world.

Though an agent of the Dragon, the scope of influence and power given to the Creature from the Sea was more extensive and impressive than the Dragon himself. Again, the Creature was able to elicit worship from everyone whose name was not written in the Book of Life of the Lamb. They worship in heaven. Those who dwell on earth are the only ones who worship the Beast.

9 If any man have an ear, let him hear. 10 He that leadeth into captivity shall go into captivity: he that killeth with the sword must be killed with the sword. Here is the patience and the faith of the saints.

The words of Revelation 13:10 are derived from the prophet Jeremiah.

"And it shall come to pass, if they say unto thee, Whither shall we go forth? then thou shalt tell them, Thus saith the Lord; Such as are for death, to death; and such as are for the sword, to the sword; and such as are for the famine, to the famine; and such as are for the captivity, to the captivity" (Jer. 15:2).

"And when he cometh, he shall smite the land of Egypt, and deliver such as are for death to death; and such as are for captivity to captivity; and such as are for the sword to the sword (Jer. 43:11).

> Christ has a chosen remnant, redeemed by his blood, recorded in his book, sealed by his Spirit; and though the devil and antichrist may overcome the body, and

> take away the natural life, they cannot conquer the soul, nor prevail with true believers to forsake their Saviour, and join his enemies. Perseverance in the faith of the gospel and true worship of God, in this great hour of trial and temptation, which would deceive all but the elect, is the character of those registered in the book of life. This powerful motive and encouragement to constancy, is the great design of the whole Revelation[1]

The promise of God is that the saints will endure, they will have patience, and they will be given faith for the journey into grace, and glory.

The Fourth Cycle

Scene Six: The Second Beast: The Creature from the Earth: The False Prophet Brings: People to the Beast from the Sea

11 And I beheld another beast coming up out of the earth; and he had two horns like a lamb, and he spake as a dragon.

[1] Matthew Henry commenting on Revelation 13:7–8.

A Wolf in Sheep's Clothing

The Unholy Trinity is complete. The Dragon, emulates God the Father, the Creature from the Sea, emulates God the Son, and the Creature from the Earth emulates God the Holy Spirit. The Church is reminded afresh that Satan is consistently a counterfeit, and non-creative. Only God can create. Apart from God's creative work, "there is nothing new under the sun" (Eccl. 1:9).

12 **And he exerciseth all the power of the first beast before him, and causeth the earth and them which dwell therein to worship the first beast, whose deadly wound was healed.**

The First Beast is the Beast from the Sea. The objective of the Second Beast, the Beast from the Earth, is to bring people to worship the First Beast, the Creature from the Sea. The way attention is drawn to the First Beast is through great wonders, or signs. One miracle in particular is to make fire come down from heaven to the earth as Elijah once did on Mt. Carmel.

> And it came to pass at the time of the offering of the evening sacrifice, that Elijah the prophet came near, and said, Lord God of Abraham, Isaac, and of Israel, let it be known this day that thou art God in Israel, and that I am thy servant, and that I have done all these things at thy word. 37 Hear me, O Lord, hear me, that this people may know that thou art the Lord God, and that thou hast turned their heart back again. 38 Then the fire of the Lord fell, and consumed the burnt sacrifice, and the wood, and the stones, and the dust, and licked up the water that was in the trench (1 Kgs. 18:36–38).

13 And he doeth great wonders, so that he maketh fire come down from heaven on the earth in the sight of men,

The great wonders (Gk. *sēmeion*; sign) that were performed by the Second Beast, the Creature from the Earth, were not authentic miracles for only Jesus could perform a true miracle. The true miracles Jesus performed validated His authentic message and ministry. "But if I do, though ye believe not me, believe the works: that ye may know, and believe, that the Father is in me, and I in him" (John 10:38). Jesus knew the power of deception and warned against it. "And many false prophets shall rise, and shall deceive many" (Matt. 24:11).

14 And deceiveth them that dwell on the earth by *the means of* those miracles which he had power to do in the sight of the beast; saying to them that dwell on the earth, that they should make an image to the beast, which had the wound by a sword, and did live.

Those who dwell on the earth are the ungodly, the unbelieving, the unregenerate. Those who dwell on earth believe the false miracles and embrace the suggestion of making an image to the First Beast, the Creature from the Sea who had seven heads, one of which was wounded, but lived. The righteous know better than to make an image of worship. "Thou shalt not make unto thee any graven image, or any likeness of anything that is in heaven above, or that is in the earth beneath, or that is in the water under the earth" (Exod. 20:4).

15 And he had power to give life unto the image of the beast, that the image of the beast should both speak, and cause that as many as would not worship the image of the beast should be killed.

By emulating the Holy Spirit, the Creature from the Earth exercises all the power of the First Beast, and then energizes him by allowing wonders, or signs to be performed in order to deceive "them that dwell on the earth," a reference to those whose names are not in the Book of Life. Anyone who does not worship the image of the Beast from the Sea was to be executed.

16 **And he causeth all, both small and great, rich and poor, free and bond, to receive a mark in their right hand, or in their foreheads:**

Here is the ungodly counterfeiting of the sealing of God's elect which is set forth in Revelation 7:3 and Revelation 9:3.

17 **And that no man might buy or sell, save he that had the mark, or the name of the beast, or the number of his name.**

To confirm loyalty to the Beast from the Sea, a mark was placed on the right hand, and in the forehead of those who worshipped the First Beast. The name of the Beast is given by the number, 666, or six hundred threescore and six.

Look for a Number, Not a Name

18 **Here is wisdom. Let him that hath understanding count the number of the beast: for it is the number of a man; and his number *is* Six hundred threescore *and* six.**

John said it is possible to count, or calculate the number, not the name, of the Beast from the Sea, if a person has wisdom.

Keep in mind that John is explaining a symbol. The Beast is really a man, says John, and any person who has understanding can calculate, the number of the First Beast, or the Beast from the Sea, because understanding what is being communicated here is not a special spiritual gift. "Wisdom resteth in the heart of him that hath understanding" (Prov. 14:33).

Those who read, those who heard the words of Revelation read in the first century were called upon to figure out the statement. Therefore, the Revelation *cannot* be a cryptic reference to anyone beyond the first century, and certainly to no one in the twenty-first century or beyond.

God does not mock His regenerated people with commandments they cannot obey by His power, and by His Spirit. Therefore, "let him that hath understanding," understand. In particular, understand that the Beast in view is to be known and identified all through history. There is no time in the life of the Church where the main message of the Revelation cannot be understood.

If that is true, then why is there so much controversy over this passage?

Part of the answer to that inquiry is found in an abiding temptation that is succumbed to time and again.

The temptation comes to the Church in every generation to engage in gematria calculation, or assigning a numerical value to a name, word, or phrase. This practice was embraced by the Assyrians, Babylonians, Greeks, and Jews.

In context, regarding Revelation 13:18, the thought comes that if the right name can be found, and a numerical value is assigned to each letter in the name so that the total will be six hundred and sixty-six, there will be confirmation of the identity of the First Beast, or the Creature from the Sea. The identity of the Antichrist can be known.

If the temptation to engage in gematria is restrained, and the Church remembers that seven is the number of perfection in Revelation, then what John is simply saying is that the First Beast, the Beast from the Sea, the Beast that is energized by another spirit, the Beast that demands worship, is a man who falls short of perfection. The Beast is not God, no matter how hard he tries.

That is the message of affirmation the Church needs to hear in every century so the saints can say, "OUR GOD REIGNS!"

No Beast, no man, can dominate the people of God.

The early Christians understood, and so can others. Because the believer resides in the heavenlies, there is no power on earth that can harm the saint, ultimately. The most any Beast, any Man, any political or religious figure can do, is send a Christian to glory. But even in that, the Beast remains what it is, always short of perfection, honor, divine power, and majesty.

The good news about Revelation 13:18 is that what John is saying is not a mystery. The Beast in view is not difficult to discern, or understand.

The Beast of Revelation 13:18 is not someone in the eighteenth century to be known by the French, who thought it was Napoleon as discussed in *War and Peace* by Leo Tolstoy. He is not a person to be identified in the twentieth century as Mussolini, as Dr. M. R. DeHann did, the founder of Radio Bible Class. The Beast from the Sea of Revelation 13:18 is not someone to be unveiled in the twenty-first century as Saddam Hussein, as many prophetic pundits did, before the Middle Eastern dictator was executed on Saturday, December 30, 2006. Even after the tyrant of Iraqi was executed, headlines around the world still asked, "Is Saddam Hussein Dead or Still Alive?"

The obsession of not a few Christians with current events, driven by vivid imaginations, and a theological system which promotes sensationalism, misses the simple teaching of Scripture, that could be a source of comfort to the Church in every generation. The Beast is but a man. Man will never be perfect. Man will never be God. To understand this is wisdom. Let him that hath understanding, hear what the Spirit has to say.

Revelation Chapter 14

The Fourth Cycle

Scene Seven

1 And I looked, and, lo, a Lamb stood on the mount Sion, and with him an hundred forty *and* four thousand, having his Father's name written in their foreheads.

Since this is the only reference to Mount Sion in Revelation, it is good to ask whether this is the earthly Mount Zion, in Jerusalem, in Israel, or, is this the Heavenly Zion, the City of Our Great God. The context favors the Heavenly Zion (Heb. Tsiyon; sunny height, mountain). "But ye are come unto mount Sion, and unto the city of the living God, the heavenly Jerusalem, and to an innumerable company of angels" (Heb. 12:22). Mount Zion represent the Kingdom of God.

2 And I heard a voice from heaven, as the voice of many waters, and as the voice of a great thunder: and I heard the voice of harpers harping with their harps:

3 And they sung as it were a new song before the throne, and before the four beasts, and the elders: and no man could learn that song but the hundred *and* forty *and* four thousand, which were redeemed from the earth.

4 These are they which were not defiled with women; for they are virgins. These are they which follow the Lamb whithersoever he goeth. These were redeemed from among men, *being* the firstfruits unto God and to the Lamb.

5 And in their mouth was found no guile: for they are without fault before the throne of God.

Here is a lovely picture of praise and worship in heaven by 144,000 saints who have the Father's name written in their foreheads. In the Bible, God is given many names, such as Elohim, Adonai, Jehovah Jireh, and El Shaddai. Each name teaches something different about the Father's character. Adonai means "Lord," and reflects the authority of God over all creation. Jehovah Jireh means, "the Lord will provide."

For the 144,000 saints to have their Father's name written in their foreheads was for them to be saying something particular about Him in the place where they make decisions, their frontal lobes. There are people who have the character of God etched in their minds. In Hebrews 10:16 we read: "This is the covenant that I will make with them after those days, saith the Lord, I will put my laws into their hearts, and in their minds will I write them; And their sins and iniquities will I remember no more" (Heb. 10:16–17). To have the Father's name in the forehead is to have the Father's character on the mind to the point they are considered to be "without fault" or, "blameless" (Gk. *amōmos*; unblemished). This does not mean they were without moral fault or were perfect. It does means they were covenantally faithful.

The Fifth Cycle (14:6–20)

Scene One: The Church and the Last Judgment: The First Angel: Preaches the Gospel

6 And I saw another angel fly in the midst of heaven, having the everlasting gospel to preach unto them that dwell on the earth, and to every nation, and kindred, and tongue, and people,

Time and again the grace of God precedes the judgment of God. There is a call to repentance before the terror of the Lord is administered. John saw an angel preach to "them that dwell on the earth," a reference to the ungodly. The message of repentance is for every nation, tribe, language, and people.

A truth is established. When judgment comes, it does not come to those who have never had a chance to love God and obey Him, because God has shown the truth to all. Romans 1:18–20 explains.

> For the wrath of God is revealed from heaven against all ungodliness and unrighteousness of men, who hold the truth in unrighteousness; Because that which may be known of God is manifest in them; for God hath shewed it unto them. For the invisible things of him from the creation of the world are clearly seen, being understood by the things that are made, even his eternal power and Godhead; so that they are without excuse.

Creation preaches the gospel. It bears witness to the Creator. Therefore, no one will be able to say, "I never had a chance to know the Lord."

7 Saying with a loud voice, Fear God, and give glory to him; for the hour of his judgment is come: and worship him that made heaven, and earth, and the sea, and the fountains of waters.

The two facets of gospel repentance mentioned are, fear of God, and giving Him glory. It is good news to tell people that God shows grace and mercy to those who honor Him with a sense of respect, awe, and submission to His known will. Those who have a dread and terror of divine judgment, hell, and God's omnipotence are not foolish, but wise. "The fear of the Lord is the beginning of wisdom" (Prov. 9:10), not the termination of wisdom. Therefore, give God the glory. Speak well of Him. Do not blaspheme His holy name.

The Second Angel Announces the Fall of Babylon

8 And there followed another angel, saying, Babylon is fallen, is fallen, that great city, because she made all nations drink of the wine of the wrath of her fornication.

This is the first time Babylon is mentioned in Revelation. It appears as a judged city, because it has filled the earth with acts of sexual immorality. Later in the Revelation, Babylon will appear as great, and mysterious. It does not matter. In the end, Babylon is fallen. Babylon is the representation of political power that is morally corrupt, leading to unspeakable acts of sensual improprieties. However powerful Babylon may be, she is fallen. However large and intimidating any political power may become in any generation, when it does not give God the glory, it will be judged, it will collapse, it will fall.

In Isaiah 13:17–20 the prophet said that Babylon would be destroyed and never rebuilt. The prophet was not wrong. Today, Babylon is still an empty city. After the 2003 invasion of Iraq, the military forces of the United States built a military base on the ruins of Babylon. If there is a future Babylon to be rebuilt then John would be contradicting Isaiah, and that cannot happen. God is not a man that He should lie (Num. 23:19).

The message of John is that any great but corrupt military or political power that seeks to harm the Church will be destroyed. This is a constant theme in Revelation. In order to comfort the Church in every generation it needs to be repeated time and again.

The Third Angel Warns of God's Wrath

[9] And the third angel followed them, saying with a loud voice, If any man worship the beast and his image, and receive *his* mark in his forehead, or in his hand, [10] The same shall drink of the wine of the wrath of God, which is poured out without mixture into the cup of his indignation; and he shall be tormented with fire and brimstone in the presence of the holy angels, and in the presence of the Lamb: [11] And the smoke of their torment ascendeth up for ever and ever: and they have no rest day nor night, who worship the beast and his image, and whosoever receiveth the mark of his name. [12] Here is the patience of the saints: here *are* they that keep the commandments of God, and the faith of Jesus.

The word for patience (Gk. *hupomonē*) refers to a cheerful (or hopeful) endurance, constancy. It is a promise that is in view here for those that keep the commandments of God, and the faith of Jesus. The promise is that the wicked shall suffer, and the righteous shall be rewarded. That is the believers hope. The Puritan William Gurnall noted, "Truly, hope is the saints covering, wherein he wraps himself, when he lays his body down to sleep in the grave: 'My flesh,' saith David, 'shall rest in hope.'"

A Voice from Heaven

13 And I heard a voice from heaven saying unto me, Write, Blessed *are* the dead which die in the Lord from henceforth: Yea, saith the Spirit, that they may rest from their labours; and their works do follow them.

Eternity alone can determine what long lasting effects a person who loves God and lives for Jesus will have. One generation will bless the next until the end of time.

14 And I looked, and behold a white cloud, and upon the cloud *one* sat like unto the Son of man, having on his head a golden crown, and in his hand a sharp sickle.

The Fourth Angel Demands a Harvest: The First Sharp Sickle: The Gathering of the Elect

15 And another angel came out of the temple, crying with a loud voice to him that sat on the cloud, Thrust in thy sickle, and reap: for the time is come for thee to reap; for the harvest of the earth is ripe.

The One that sat on the cloud is the Lord Jesus. He is encouraged by the angel from the Heavenly Temple to begin the harvest of the earth. The hour of final judgment has come. But first, Jesus must have a harvest of His own. He will gather the elect to Himself.

16 **And he that sat on the cloud thrust in his sickle on the earth; and the earth was reaped.**

There is a parable Jesus told that parallels the scene John witnesses in Revelation.

> And he said, So is the kingdom of God, as if a man should cast seed into the ground; And should sleep, and rise night and day, and the seed should spring and grow up, he knoweth not how. For the earth bringeth forth fruit of herself; first the blade, then the ear, after that the full corn in the ear. But when the fruit is brought forth, immediately he putteth in the sickle, because the harvest is come (Mark 4:26–29).

The Fifth Angel: A Second Sharp Sickle

17 **And another angel came out of the temple which is in heaven, he also having a sharp sickle.**

The Sixth Angel with Power over Fire: The Third Sharp Sickle: The Judgment of the Wicked

18 **And another angel came out from the altar, which had power over fire; and cried with a loud cry to him that had the sharp sickle, saying, Thrust in thy sharp sickle, and gather the clusters of the vine of the earth; for her grapes**

are fully ripe. [19] And the angel thrust in his sickle into the earth, and gathered the vine of the earth, and cast *it* into the great winepress of the wrath of God. [20] And the winepress was trodden without the city, and blood came out of the winepress, even unto the horse bridles, by the space of a thousand *and* six hundred furlongs.

The image is that of a crushing judgment under the winepress of the wrath of God. Outside the Holy City of Jerusalem was a bloodbath. The slaughter of the wicked was so great, a river of blood flowed as high as a horses bridle, or about five and a half feet tall, for 1,600 furlongs (Gk. stadion), or about 184 miles long.

The parallel is between Jesus, whose death took place outside the Holy City of Jerusalem, and the judgment of the wicked, who shall have their part in Gehenna. The Valley of Gehenna was outside the Holy City. Those who reject Jesus must die outside the city, and bear their own judgment.

When individuals reject God's plan of salvation for their own, that judgment is allowed to take place. Either a person is judged by God in Christ, with sin being covered and forgiven because the penalty has been paid, or a person is crushed under the guilt of their own sin.

Revelation Chapter 15

The Sixth Cycle (15:1—16:21)

Scene One: The Seven Last Plagues

**1 And I saw another sign in heaven, great and marvel-
lous, seven angels having the seven last plagues; for in
them is filled up the wrath of God.**

Back in the Heavenly Temple

**2 And I saw as it were a sea of glass mingled with fire:
and them that had gotten the victory over the beast, and
over his image, and over his mark, *and* over the number of
his name, stand on the sea of glass, having the harps of
God. 3 And they sing the song of Moses the servant of
God, and the song of the Lamb, saying, Great and marvel-
lous *are* thy works, Lord God Almighty; just and true *are*
thy ways, thou King of saints.**

The Old and New Testament are united in Revelation, for God has one people, one plan of redemption, one glorious program of victory for His one Church, whose Foundation is Jesus Christ our Lord.

[4] Who shall not fear thee, O Lord, and glorify thy name? For *thou* only *art* holy: for all nations shall come and worship before thee; for thy judgments are made manifest.

Those who worship in the Heavenly Temple cannot imagine anyone not fearing the Lord and worshipping Him. Indeed, in one sense it is true. Though the heart is incredibly sinful, wicked, and hard, the Creator knows how to move, so that one day, every knee shall bow, and every tongue shall confess that Jesus is Lord to the glory of God (Rom. 14:11). People do know that God alone is holy, just, and good. Those in heaven know this. Those in Hell know this too.

The Sixth Cycle

Scene Two

[5] And after that I looked, and, behold, the temple of the tabernacle of the testimony in heaven was opened: [6] And the seven angels came out of the temple, having the seven plagues, clothed in pure and white linen, and having their breasts girded with golden girdles.

As Moses came from the presence of God to administer God's judgment on Egypt, so the angels from the Heavenly Temple carried the seven plagues to administer judgment on earth.

[7] And one of the four beasts gave unto the seven angels seven golden vials full of the wrath of God, who liveth for ever and ever.

The prayers of the martyred saints, carried by angels in golden bowls in Revelation 4:8, have ascended to heaven. Holy Angels have filled those golden bowls with answered prayers in the form of seven last plague, full of the wrath of God, and reminiscent of the plagues that fell on Egypt.

Plagues on Egypt	Revelation Plagues
Blood (Exod. 7:14–24)	Sores (Rev. 16:2)
Frogs (Exod. 7:25—8:15)	Sea turned to blood (Rev. 16:3)
Gnats (Exod. 8:16 – 19	Rivers turn to blood (Rev. 16:4, 7)
Flies (Exod. 8:20 – 32)	Sun Scorches (Rev. 16:8, 9)
Livestock (Exod. 9:1–7)	Political upheaval (Rev. 16:10, 11)
Boils (Exod. 9:8–12)	Euphrates dried (Rev. 16:12–16)
Hail (Exod. 9:13–35)	Cosmic changes (Rev. 16:17–21)
Locusts (Exod. 10:1–20)	
Darkness (Exod. 10:21–29)	
Death (Exod. 11:1–10; 12:29–32)	

8 **And the temple was filled with smoke from the glory of God, and from his power; and no man was able to enter into the temple, till the seven plagues of the seven angels were fulfilled.**

Revelation Chapter 16

The Sixth Cycle

Scene Three

[1] **And I heard a great voice out of the temple saying to the seven angels, Go your ways, and pour out the vials of the wrath of God upon the earth.**

The Great Commission, is the commission of Christ to proclaim the good news of the gospel. Here is another Great Commission, but it is to proclaim great judgment upon the earth.

The First Bowl Judgment: Painful Sores

[2] **And the first went, and poured out his vial upon the earth; and there fell a noisome and grievous sore upon the men which had the mark of the beast, and *upon* them which worshipped his image.**

The Second Bowl Judgment: Blood in the Sea

3 And the second angel poured out his vial upon the sea; and it became as the blood of a dead *man:* and every living soul died in the sea.

The Third Bowl Judgment: Rivers of Blood

4 And the third angel poured out his vial upon the rivers and fountains of waters; and they became blood.

Death follows the flowing waters of blood, as the fresh waters that sustain life are polluted.

5 And I heard the angel of the waters say, Thou art righteous, O Lord, which art, and wast, and shalt be, because thou hast judged thus.

Once man begins to stand in judgment on the justice of God, the God of revelation is eventually reduced to a God of human imagination, who is no better, stronger, or wiser than mortal man. Hell is dismissed, diminished, or denied, and every single thought and action is idealized to the point that there is no right or wrong. Let the Church say with the angels, "Thou art righteous, O Lord, *because* You have judged as You have."

The Righteous are Vindicated

6 For they have shed the blood of saints and prophets, and thou hast given them blood to drink; for they are worthy.

One of the great moral questions of the Bible is whether or not God is just when He severely judges the sins of men. Will God give the righteous, "blood to drink?" "Will the Martyred

Saints and Prophets be vindicated? The question is anticipated in Scripture, and answered.

7 **And I heard another out of the altar say, Even so, Lord God Almighty, true and righteous *are* thy judgments.**

All the judgments of God are true and righteous. The wicked have persecuted and executed without mercy the righteous, including the Martyred Souls of those under the altar. In perfect righteousness and justice God will execute the wicked without mercy. God has given the righteous, "blood to drink," for they are worthy. The justice of God satisfies the thirst for justice of the Martyred Saints. There is no sentimentality in prefect justice. Justice is not to be mitigated, but affirmed.

The Fourth Bowl Judgment: Scorching Heat from the Sun

8 **And the fourth angel poured out his vial upon the sun; and power was given unto him to scorch men with fire.**
9 **And men were scorched with great heat, and blasphemed the name of God, which hath power over these plagues: and they repented not to give him glory.**

Having said that God knows how to elicit praise from the ungodly, John notices that it does not last. When the fourth plague is administered, and ungodly individuals were scorched with heat, they cursed God, blasphemed His name, and repented not to give Him glory. If that is true because earths sun grows warm, how much greater is the cursing and blasphemy that takes place in Hell where the fire is never quenched? Those under the wrath of God are foolish not to repent.

Thomas Boston said, "That which a man spits against heaven, shall fall back on his own face."

The Fifth Bowl Judgment: Darkness over all the Land

10 And the fifth angel poured out his vial upon the seat of the beast; and his kingdom was full of darkness; and they gnawed their tongues for pain,

Like the plague that fell on Egypt during the days of Moses and the Pharaoh (Exod. 10:21–29), the world is plunged into darkness and despair.

11 And blasphemed the God of heaven because of their pains and their sores, and repented not of their deeds.

For the fourth time in Revelation, the observation is made that no matter how intense the judgment, no matter how severe the punishment, like a dog returning to his vomit, the sinner returns to sin, and refuses to repent of evil deeds (Rev. 2:21; 9:20; 16:9, 11).

The honest heart, the self-aware heart will confess this, for one's own life bears witness to the truth that individuals do not repent. The word brings no emotional or behavioral response, only intellectual boredom. The heart says in essence, "I have heard the call to repent—now be quiet."

God has given many Royal Commands which are disobeyed, no matter what sickness, sorrow, hardship, or loss is extracted in life. The Bible says that if we would stand in judgment upon ourselves, we should not be judged. But rather than condemn self, the heart is prone simply to move on without any bothering to justify behavior. The will to power, and the principle of pleasure, is enough to make a person do what God has forbidden.

Like Pharaoh of Egypt, individuals might momentarily praise the Lord God, yet ultimately, there is no repentance. Those who pretend to repent, momentarily, should take no confidence in that moment of pseudo salvation, upon reflection.

> Beware, I pray thee, of presuming that thou art saved. If thy heart be renewed, if thou shalt hate the things that thou didst once love, and love the things that thou didst once hate; if thou hast really repented; if there be a thorough change of mind in thee; if thou be born again, then hast thou reason to rejoice: but if there be no vital change, no inward godliness; if there be no love to God, no prayer, no work of the Holy Spirit, then thy saying "I am saved" is but thine own assertion, and it may delude, but it will not deliver thee (Charles Spurgeon).

The Sixth Bowl Judgment: The Drying of the Euphrates River: An Army from the East

12 And the sixth angel poured out his vial upon the great river Euphrates; and the water thereof was dried up, that the way of the kings of the east might be prepared.

Historically, many of the enemies of God's people came from the North, and the East, to include Edom, Moab, Amon, the Assyrians, Babylonians, and the Medes-Persians. The larger image, is that the enemies of God come against the people of God, only to fail to destroy them. Political power is used to come against God's people, religious power is used to hurt them, economic forces are used against them, and religion is used to hurt the Lord's anointed, but to no avail. The Church lives. "*Our God reigns!*"

THE SIXTH CYCLE

Scene Four: Three Frogs from the Unholy Trinity

13 And I saw three unclean spirits like frogs *come* out of the mouth of the dragon, and out of the mouth of the beast, and out of the mouth of the false prophet.

The Unholy Trinity consists of the Dragon, the Beast from the Sea, and the Beast from the Earth, which is the False Prophet.

14 For they are the spirits of devils, working miracles, *which* go forth unto the kings of the earth and of the whole world, to gather them to the battle of that great day of God Almighty.

In their collective foolishness, the kings of the earth can talk themselves into a state of war through false bravado. However, in the hour of actual conflict they are nothing before God. History repeats itself, because basic human nature does not change. "And the kings of the earth, and the great men, and the rich men, and the chief captains, and the mighty men, and every bondman, and every free man, hid themselves in the dens and in the rocks of the mountains; And said to the mountains and rocks, Fall on us, and hide us from the face of him that sitteth on the throne, and from the wrath of the Lamb: For the great day of his wrath is come; and who shall be able to stand?" (Rev. 6:15–17). When the Battle of Armageddon is supposed to take place, there is no battle!

The Sixth Cycle

Scene Five: A Dramatic Pause: The Prelude to Armageddon

15 Behold, I come as a thief. Blessed *is* he that watcheth, and keepeth his garments, lest he walk naked, and they see his shame.

John remembered the words of Jesus telling Christians how to get ready for His Second Advent. Jesus is coming the second time for all who believe (Heb. 9:28). He will come in the same manner as He went away. This means that when the Lord suddenly appears, like a thief in the night, His presence will be known in a visible manner (Acts 1:11). A thief in the antient world came suddenly, and with great force upon the victim, and not in a sneaky way, like many thieves today. The Christian must get ready for the Battle of Armageddon. How is the Church to make herself ready?

John says to the Church, in essence, "In preparation for Armageddon, keep your garments clean." In other words, be holy. Christians prepare for battle by putting on the whole armor of God. The saints do not arm themselves with rifles, bazookas, tanks, mortars, and a trained military presence with men and deadly machines on the land, in the air, and on the seas. The best preparation is a holy life.

If the kings of the East are on the march, crossing a dried-up Euphrates River to arrive at the Valley of Jezreel to await the arrival of the Lord of Hosts, then obviously the Lord cannot come as a thief in the night. Therefore, the *vision* of spiritual truth is to convey what Jesus has always taught, and that is, the end does not come with observation.

It is futile to look for "signs of the times."

It is foolish to appeal to current events as proof that the world is now in "the last days."

It is irresponsible for Christian writers to talk about living in the terminal generation, as if there are not more children to be born, and more centuries to pass. There are spiritual truths to learn from the vision of Revelation.

There are spiritual realities of which to be reminded: Specifically, Christians are to watch, if they want to be blessed. The Church is to keep her garments pure, if she wants to be holy. Believers are to be clothed in righteousness, if they do not want others to see their shame.

The end of time will be marked by the unexpected return of Jesus. The way to get ready for the end is to live a life of righteousness. Blessed is the Christian who stays awake in the service of the Lord, and does not fall asleep while on duty.

Here is the prelude to Armageddon. It involves Christians living life *coram Deo*, before the face of God. It consists of the Church getting ready to greet, and receive the King of kings, and Lord of lords.

When the King comes, He will find faith on the earth.

When the King comes, there will be no battle, for the Lord will consume His enemies with the breath of His mouth. "And then shall that Wicked be revealed, whom the Lord shall consume with the spirit of his mouth, and shall destroy with the brightness of his coming" (2 Thess. 2:8).

THE SIXTH CYCLE

Scene Seven: A Prelude to Armageddon

[16] And he gathered them together into a place called in the Hebrew tongue Armageddon.

This is the only time Armageddon (Gk. "mountain of Megiddo") is mentioned in Revelation, with an amazing observation. Though the wicked are gathered spiritually, no battle takes place. Historically, this was not the case. Armageddon was the scene of many historic battles.

Though Bible scholars disagree, it is possible that Armageddon was situated in the valley between Mount Carmel and the city of Jezreel. Known as the Valley of Zezreel, or the Plain of Esdraelon, it was associated with the good king, Josiah, who was killed there. Josiah was caught up in the conflict between Egypt and Assyria. Josiah sided with the Assyrians against Pharaoh-Nechoh, king of Egypt. That political and military alignment cost him his life.

> Now the rest of the acts of Josiah, and all that he did, are they not written in the book of the chronicles of the kings of Judah? In his days Pharaoh–Nechoh king of Egypt went up against the king of Assyria to the river Euphrates: and king Josiah went against him; and he slew him at Megiddo, when he had seen him. And his servants carried him in a chariot dead from Megiddo, and brought him to Jerusalem, and buried him in his own sepulcher (2 Kgs. 23:28–30a).

In Revelation, the historical site known as Armageddon represented a place where super power met on the field of battle.

However, when the Unholy Trinity tries to engage God as an equal superpower, there is no battle, it is no contest.

The reason why there is no battle at Armageddon is because no one can fight against God. The Devil can make war in heaven, and fight Michael and other angels. The Devil can make war on the saints. The Devil can make war on the nations. But neither the Devil, the Beast from the Sea, nor the Beast from the Earth can fight against God. There can be a gathering for conflict, but it does not matter. The war is over before it begins. There is no battle. Everything that man believes to be powerful, awesome, and dangerous, is nothing before the presence of the Lord.

The Sixth Cycle

Scene Eight: The Seventh Bowl Judgment: Cosmic Changes

17 And the seventh angel poured out his vial into the air; and there came a great voice out of the temple of heaven, from the throne, saying, It is done.

When Jesus died at Calvary, He cried out, "It is finished!" (John 19:30). With the pouring out of the last judgment, a voice from the Heavenly Temple cried out, "It is done." Either Christ completes the work of salvation, or sinners endure the wrath of God until justice is satisfied.

**18 And there were voices, and thunders, and lightnings;
and there was a great earthquake, such as was not since
men were upon the earth, so mighty an earthquake, *and* so
great. 19 And the great city was divided into three parts,
and the cities of the nations fell: and great Babylon came**

in remembrance before God, to give unto her the cup of the wine of the fierceness of his wrath.

Jesus once drank from the cup of God's wrath. He pleaded not to, but then submitted to the will of the Father. "And he went a little further, and fell on his face, and prayed, saying, O my Father, if it be possible, let this cup pass from me: nevertheless, not as I will, but as thou wilt" (Matt. 26:39).

Spiritually, Christians drink from the same cup of the Lord, with this difference. The cup of bitterness has become the cup of blessing. "The cup of blessing which we bless, is it not the communion of the blood of Christ?" (1 Cor. 10:16). Indeed, it is.

Those who refuse to drink from the cup of Christ, will have their own cup to drink of the wrath of God, illustrated symbolically by Great Babylon.

20 **And every island fled away, and the mountains were not found.**

A Judgment of Hail

21 **And there fell upon men a great hail out of heaven, *every stone* about the weight of a talent: and men blasphemed God because of the plague of the hail; for the plague thereof was exceeding great.**

The Bible says, it is a dreadful thing to fall into the hands of the living God who is angry with the wicked (Heb. 10:31). John conveys the wrath of God, as he sees in his vision how easily it is for God to shake the earth, and destroy everything, and everyone in it. The end of God's wrath against those who dwell on the earth, those who are ungodly, is to destroy everything.

In apocalyptic language, when God moves in judgment, islands vanish. Mountains are not found. There is cosmic chaos. Stones of hail fall from heaven weighing no less than 80 pounds. Men blaspheme God in their pain and suffering, who only laughs. Oh! "Let all the earth fear the LORD: let all the inhabitants of the world stand in awe of him" (Ps. 33:8).

The judgment of hailstones John witnesses alludes to the judgment of hailstones rained on Egypt by Moses, with the same end result.

Grace Precedes Judgement

"Then the Lord said unto Moses, Go in unto Pharaoh, and tell him, Thus saith the Lord God of the Hebrews, Let my people go, that they may serve me. . . . Behold, tomorrow about this time I will cause it to rain a very grievous hail, such as hath not been in Egypt since the foundation thereof even until now. Send therefore now, and gather thy cattle, and all that thou hast in the field; for upon every man and beast which shall be found in the field, and shall not be brought home, the hail shall come down upon them, and they shall die . . ."

Judgment Falls

"And Moses went out of the city from Pharaoh, and spread abroad his hands unto the Lord: and the thunders and hail ceased, and the rain was not poured upon the earth. And when Pharaoh saw that the rain and the hail and the thunders were ceased, he sinned yet more, and hardened his heart, he and his servants."

The Heart is Hardened

"And the heart of Pharaoh was hardened, neither would he let the children of Israel go; as the Lord had spoken by Moses" (Exod. 9:1, 18–19, 33–35).

The Cycle of Sin and Grace was manifested in the days of Moses, repeated in the days of John, and will continue until the end of time. Individuals will blaspheme God, and curse their fate on earth. Meanwhile, those who dwell in the Heavenlies will rejoice their prayers are being answered, justice is being administered, the wicked do not prevail, there will be a final judgment, and God cannot be opposed, let alone overthrown or deposed. "*Our God reigns!*"

Revelation Chapter 17

THE SEVENTH CYCLE (17:1—22:5)

The Longest Cycle: The Beginning of the Cycle

A Description of Mystery Babylon: The First Great Woman

Scene One: The Great Whore

1 And there came one of the seven angels which had the
seven vials, and talked with me, saying unto me, Come
hither; I will shew unto thee the judgment of the great
whore that sitteth upon many waters: 2 With whom the
kings of the earth have committed fornication, and the inhabitants of the earth have been made drunk with the wine
of her fornication.

Scene Two: The Great Whore Rides a Scarlet Beast

3 So he carried me away in the spirit into the wilderness:
and I saw a woman sit upon a scarlet coloured beast, full
of names of blasphemy, having seven heads and ten horns.

The Colors in Revelation

• Rainbow Colors	Rev. 4:3; 10:1
• Black	Rev. 6:5, 12
• Red	Rev. 6:4, 12; 8:8; 12:3
• Scarlet / Purple	Rev. 17:1–9
• Yellow (Gold)	Rev. 17:4
• Green	Rev. 6:8; 8:7; 9:4
• White	Rev. 3:4–5; 4:4; 7:9, 13–14; 19:14
• Jewel Tones	Rev. 4; 21:9–27

4 **And the woman was arrayed in purple and scarlet colour, and decked with gold and precious stones and pearls, having a golden cup in her hand full of abominations and filthiness of her fornication:**

There is some irony in the image. The greater the effort for the woman to look elegant, sophisticated, and fashionable, the greater was her detestation, her moral impurity, and her sexual appetites, which included adultery and incest.

5 **And upon her forehead *was* a name written, MYSTERY, BABYLON THE GREAT, THE MOTHER OF HARLOTS AND ABOMINATIONS OF THE EARTH.**

The image of a name written on the forehead was familiar to the Jews, for the High Priest wore a mitre. At the front of the mitre was a signet, a stone. On the stone was written, HOLINESS TO THE LORD.

> And thou shalt make a plate of pure gold, and grave upon it, like the engravings of a signet, HOLINESS TO THE Lord. And thou shalt put it on a blue lace, that it may be upon the mitre; upon the forefront of the mitre

> it shall be. And it shall be upon Aarons forehead, that Aaron may bear the iniquity of the holy things, which the children of Israel shall hallow in all their holy gifts; and it shall be always upon his forehead, that they may be accepted before the Lord (Exod. 28:36–38).

In Revelation, John sees a mockery of the holy mitre in the name written on the forehead of the Scarlet Woman. The holiness of the priest representing God, was replaced by the unholiness of the woman.

Various Names Written
On the Forehead
(Message Conveyed)

- The Name of the Father (Rev. 7:3; 9:4; 14:1)
  Holy Unto the Lord
- The Name of the Beast (Rev. 13:16; 14:9; 20:4)
  Unholy
- The Name of the Scarlet Woman (Rev. 17:5)
  Unholy
- The Name of the Lamb (Rev. 22:4)
  Holy Unto the Lord

Scene Three

6 And I saw the woman drunken with the blood of the saints, and with the blood of the martyrs of Jesus: and when I saw her, I wondered with great admiration.

Babylon does not simply represent political corruption, but spiritual evil as well. The woman was drunk with the blood of the saints, and the blood of the martyrs. In the early Church, there were many who did die for the cause of Christ. Multitudes suffered terrible deaths. The blood of the martyrs became the seed of the Church, said Tertullian (c. 155 - c. 240).

As John witnessed this scene, he became fascinated by it. "I wondered with great admiration," he confesses. At this point, the angel of heaven snapped him back to spiritual realty.

Scene Four: A Mystery Explained

7 And the angel said unto me, Wherefore didst thou marvel? I will tell thee the mystery of the woman, and of the beast that carrieth her, which hath the seven heads and ten horns. 8 The beast that thou sawest was, and is not; and shall ascend out of the bottomless pit, and go into perdition: and they that dwell on the earth shall wonder, whose names were not written in the book of life from the foundation of the world, when they behold the beast that was, and is not, and yet is.

The beast is the representation of false religion in the world. In an imitation of Christ, it is said that he "was, and is not, and yet is." Those who dwell on the earth, the ungodly, the unconverted, the non-righteous are still drawn to the beast, because their names are not written in the Book of Life.

Contrasting Christ and the Beast

Christ	The Beast
• Was, from all eternity	Was, only from his creation
• Is	Is not
• Is coming	Yet is going to destruction

A City Built on Seven Hills

[9] And here *is* the mind which hath wisdom. The seven heads are seven mountains, on which the woman sitteth.

There is, at the very least, an allusion to Rome, the city built on seven hills, which, in the first century was an expression of Babylon. Rome was filled with glory, and decadence, just like the woman. Rome was a city filled with false religions, including Caesar Worship. By noting seven *mountains*, the message is conveyed that there will be other "great whores" in the earth, reflecting the power, glory, and immorality of ancient Babylon.

The Falls of Babylon

[10] And there are seven kings: five are fallen, and one is, *and* the other is not yet come; and when he cometh, he must continue a short space. [11] And the beast that was, and is not, even he is the eighth, and is of the seven, and goeth into perdition. [12] And the ten horns which thou sawest are ten kings, which have received no kingdom as yet; but receive power as kings one hour with the beast.

In Revelation, sequence is not always for chronology, or specific enumeration, but for expansion and elaboration. Babylon *is* ten kings. The ten kings speak of all the kings that shall rule over those who dwell on the earth to lead nations into sin, and judgment. Worldly kings have one mind, and that is to give their power and strength to the beast.

[13] These have one mind, and shall give their power and strength unto the beast.

Time and again rulers sell their souls to the devil. Time and again the Evil One takes individuals to a high mountain and shows them all the kingdoms of the world and their glory. Then Satan says, "If you will fall down and worship me, I will give you all this." This offer was made to Jesus, who turned Satan down (Matt. 4:8–9).

14 These shall make war with the Lamb, and the Lamb shall overcome them: for he is Lord of lords, and King of kings: and they that are with him *are* called, and chosen, and faithful.

No matter how many kinds appear, no matter how many unite against the Lord and His saints, they shall all be defeated. They may be born of their father the Devil (Dragon), they may be his favorite child (Beast), they may be energized by an unholy but power spirit (False Prophet), the Lamb shall overcome them all. Why? Because He is Lord of lords. Jesus is King of kings. And those who follow the Lamb are the called of God. They are chosen by God. They are faithful to the end. The kings of the earth do not matter much, for they only have an hour. Each one only has a short, a very short period of time, and then it is over for them. Their eternity in hell begins.

Have you been called to the Lamb? Have you been chosen by the Lamb? Are you faithful to the Lamb? You will be if you have been *given* to the Lamb by the Father.

The Waters are Explained

15 And he saith unto me, The waters which thou sawest, where the whore sitteth, are peoples, and multitudes, and nations, and tongues. 16 And the ten horns which thou

sawest upon the beast, these shall hate the whore, and shall make her desolate and naked, and shall eat her flesh, and burn her with fire. [17] For God hath put in their hearts to fulfil his will, and to agree, and give their kingdom unto the beast, until the words of God shall be fulfilled. [18] And the woman which thou sawest is that great city, which reigneth over the kings of the earth.

One of the great restraints on political power, is God who directly puts it into the hearts of men, even evil men, to do His will. Normally, people fight and devour each other. Nations devour other nations by political intrigue, military aggression, deceitful promises, and threats. Suddenly these power rulers and nations are overthrown, as the Church watches in amazement. It is not always that better rulers take the place but for a time, there is religious reprieve for the saints. The Biblical proverb is proven true. "Whoso diggeth a pit shall fall therein: and he that rolleth a stone, it will return upon him" (Prov. 26:27).

By confusing the minds of the rulers on earth, by putting in their hearts to fulfill His will, by causing rulers to foolishly give their kingdoms to the beast, until the words of God shall be fulfilled, is how God is able to laugh at the wicked. "The Lord shall laugh at him: for he seeth that his day is coming" (Ps. 37:13). "He that sitteth in the heavens shall laugh: the Lord shall have them in derision" (Ps. 2:4).

Revelation Chapter 18

THE SEVENTH CYCLE

Scene Five: Babylon the Great is Fallen

[1] **And after these things I saw another angel come down from heaven, having great power; and the earth was lightened with his glory.**
[2] And he cried mightily with a strong voice, saying, Babylon the great is fallen, is fallen, and is become the habitation of devils, and the hold of every foul spirit, and a cage of every unclean and hateful bird.

That Babylon is great has already been stated. Babylon was great in military might. The Evil Empire was able to conquer other nations, including Israel. Babylon was great in building projects. One of the Seven Wonders of the Ancient World was found in Babylon. Babylon was great in wealth. The resources of other nations flowed into her coffers. Babylon was great in political power. Her leaders spoke, and the heads of states listened. Babylon was great in sin. She became the dwelling place for demons, a refuge for every unclean spirit, and a haven for every despicable person.

[3] **For all nations have drunk of the wine of the wrath of her fornication, and the kings of the earth have committed**

fornication with her, and the merchants of the earth are waxed rich through the abundance of her delicacies. [4] And I heard another voice from heaven, saying, Come out of her, my people, that ye be not partakers of her sins, and that ye receive not of her plagues.

Throughout history, God has called His people to come out and be separate. Abram was called out of Ur of the Chaldees. Moses and the Israelites were called out of Egypt. The Church is called out of the world. If the people of God do not partake of the sins of the wicked, they need not suffer the plagues that will fall on the unrighteous.

This is not a call for a physical separation, because it is the known will of our Lord not to be taken out of the world. "I pray not that thou shouldest take them out of the world, but that thou shouldest keep them from the evil" (John 17:15). The call from heaven is to not love the world, or the things that are in the world (1 John 2:15). The Christian is to be removed from self-centered indulgence, and others sins.

[5] For her sins have reached unto heaven, and God hath remembered her iniquities.

Sin reaches unto heaven, because God has not turned His back on His creation. The universe has not been established to run solely on natural laws. There is a moral dimension that permeates creation, leaving every person without excuse for not doing what is right.

[6] Reward her even as she rewarded you, and double unto her double according to her works: in the cup which she hath filled fill to her double. [7] How much she hath glorified herself, and lived deliciously, so much torment and sorrow give her: for she saith in her heart, I sit a queen,

and am no widow, and shall see no sorrow. [8] **Therefore shall her plagues come in one day, death, and mourning, and famine; and she shall be utterly burned with fire: for strong *is* the Lord God who judgeth her.**

The image set forth is one of utter desolation. Babylon the Great is representative of all that is in the world that needs to be judged.

The Transgressions of Babylon

- Babylon glorified herself
- Babylon lived in a luxurious manner
- Babylon sat in haughtiness like a queen
- Babylon engaged in fornication

Scene Six: The Lamentation over Babylon the Great

Lamentation Expressed by the Kings of the Earth

[9] **And the kings of the earth, who have committed for-**
nication and lived deliciously with her, shall bewail her,
and lament for her, when they shall see the smoke of her
burning, [10] **Standing afar off for the fear of her torment,**
saying, Alas, alas, that great city Babylon, that mighty city!
For in one hour is thy judgment come.

Lamentation Expressed by the Merchants of the Earth

[11] **And the merchants of the earth shall weep and mourn**
over her; for no man buyeth their merchandise any more:
[12] **The merchandise of gold, and silver, and precious**
stones, and of pearls, and fine linen, and purple, and silk,

and scarlet, and all thyine wood, and all manner vessels of ivory, and all manner vessels of most precious wood, and of brass, and iron, and marble, [13] And cinnamon, and odours, and ointments, and frankincense, and wine, and oil, and fine flour, and wheat, and beasts, and sheep, and horses, and chariots, and slaves, and souls of men.

The list of what the merchants were selling is long and comprehensive. Anything that could attract attention to a person's sight, hearing, touch, smell, or taste, was available for sale. Even lavish chariots and bodies were placed on the market.

One of the great charges against Christianity is that the New Testament supports slavery. That view needs to be challenged in light of this passage, and 1 Timothy 1:10. When writing to Timothy, Paul equates "men stealers" (Gk. andrapodistes; an enslaver) with the lawless and disobedient, and with the ungodly and sinners. In Revelation 18:13, it is obvious that the selling of bodies and souls of men is abhorrent, and is judged in the most severe way. It is not Christianity that debases human life, and places the bodies and souls of men on the market, but the merchants of this world, the wicked, the ungodly.

The Weeping and Wailing of the Wicked

[14] And the fruits that thy soul lusted after are departed from thee, and all things which were dainty and goodly are departed from thee, and thou shalt find them no more at all.

In a frantic search for personal happiness, everything the soul desires is taken, and shall never be found, in time, or in eternity. Fear, and weeping, and wailing will replace the life of luxury and ease that was once pursued. God knows how to give happiness, and He knows how to take happiness and joy away. "As the wicked are hurt by the best things," says William Jenkyn, "so the godly are bettered by the worst."

**15 The merchants of these things, which were made rich
by her, shall stand afar off for the fear of her torment,
weeping and wailing, 16 And saying, Alas, alas, that great
city, that was clothed in fine linen, and purple, and scarlet,
and decked with gold, and precious stones, and pearls! 17
For in one hour so great riches is come to nought. And
every shipmaster, and all the company in ships, and sailors,
and as many as trade by sea, stood afar off, 18 And cried
when they saw the smoke of her burning, saying, What *city*
is like unto this great city!**

"I cannot but look upon all the glory and dignity of this world, lands and lordships, crowns and kingdoms, even as on some brain-sick, beggarly fellow, that borrows fine clothes, and plays the part of a king or lord for an hour on a stage, and then comes down, and the sport is ended, and they are beggars again" (Richard Baxter).

Lamentation Expressed by the Sailors

19 And they cast dust on their heads, and cried, weeping and wailing, saying, Alas, alas, that great city, wherein were made rich all that had ships in the sea by reason of her costliness! For in one hour is she made desolate.

The kings of the earth, along with the merchants, and the sailors are in great distress over the sudden destruction of Babylon. In only one hour she was made desolate. While it is always tragic when a great empire falls suddenly, what is more alarming is the absence of intellectual curiosity as to why there is societal collapse. When a society is overwhelmingly godless, there is no spiritual discernment to comprehend that the fall of a great nation is grounded in divine judgment.

When individuals are not reflective, when individuals are not curious, when citizens of a nation do not consider life from a spiritual perspective, then all they can do is lament, and come to the conclusion that all the inventions of time, all that makes up human life is vanity. Soulless individuals are pursuing a shadow, and chasing the wind. Life is short. The years are fleeting, and filled with sorrows. "I have seen all the works that are done under the sun; and, behold, all is vanity and vexation of spirit" (Eccl. 1:14).

A life without God is a life without ultimate meaning or purpose. When all the gold is gone, when all the clothes are eaten by moths, when all the delicious foods are fed to the animals, when the ships go down in the sea, and everything on board is lost, then what? C. S. Lewis addressed this question on the precipice of World War II.

People were asking, "What is to be said and done when the world is at war?" "What is the sense of anything in life when the jaws of death are opening wide to devour everything?" For Lewis, the only way to make sense out of national disintegration, and life without meaning, is to remember there is something more to the human existence than sensual pleasures. There is the spiritual part of man. There is eternity to consider.

By looking beyond, ourselves humans can find Someone, and something greater than the vanities of life.[1]

The image that John portrays is a reminder that most people live for the moment, and they live for pleasure. The pursuit of personal happiness consumes individuals. Attention is focused on what to wear, what to eat, where to go, how to get power over others, and how to get more. The essence of prideful self is more. More money, more education, more cars, more clothes, a bigger house. Then, judgment comes, and it is gone in an hour. The world can only lament. The saints have a different response.

Scene Seven: The Hour of Judgment Becomes the Hour of Praise and Rejoicing

20 **Rejoice over her, *thou* heaven, and *ye* holy apostles and prophets; for God hath avenged you on her.**

In verse 19 there is a final collective voice of lamentation over the destruction of Babylon. This final wail of woe is then followed by another voice, a single voice, a righteous voice telling those in heaven to rejoice. The contrast is clear. The wicked weep, while the righteous rejoice. In addition, the judgment of the wicked satisfies justice. Their faithfulness to the Lord is vindicated. That is the message of the Seventh Cycle, Scene Seven of Revelation.

---

[1] C. S. Lewis, "Learning in War-Time," in *The Weight of Glory and Other Addresses*, New York: MacMillan, 1949.

Scene Eight: A Great Millstone Cast into the Sea

**[21] And a mighty angel took up a stone like a great mill-
stone, and cast *it* into the sea, saying, Thus with violence
shall that great city Babylon be thrown down, and shall be
found no more at all. [22] And the voice of harpers, and mu-
sicians, and of pipers, and trumpeters, shall be heard no
more at all in thee; and no craftsman, of whatsoever craft
he be, shall be found any more in thee; and the sound of a
millstone shall be heard no more at all in thee; [23] And the
light of a candle shall shine no more at all in thee; and the
voice of the bridegroom and of the bride shall be heard no
more at all in thee: for thy merchants were the great men
of the earth; for by thy sorceries were all nations deceived.
[24] And in her was found the blood of prophets, and of
saints, and of all that were slain upon the earth.**

Babylon was destroyed because she had given herself to sorcery, meaning people were taught not to look to God, not to honor the Lord, not to follow the Lamb, but to eat, drink, and be merry. There is a philosophy of this world that brings utter ruin and destruction on individuals, and on nations. Human philosophies, human points of view are called deceptions. The philosophies may be enhancing to listen to, but the deception is present to damn the soul for all eternity. The wisdom of this world will lead individuals to spill the blood of the righteous. One reason why there must be a day of ultimate judgment, the reason why there must be a payday, someday, for the wicked, is because of the blood of prophets, and saints, and the needless slaughter of those upon the earth.

Revelation Chapter 19

The Seventh Cycle

Scene Nine: The Triumph of God and His People

1 And after these things I heard a great voice of much
people in heaven, saying, Alleluia; Salvation, and glory,
and honour, and power, unto the Lord our God: 2 For true
and righteous *are* his judgments: for he hath judged the
great whore, which did corrupt the earth with her fornica-
tion, and hath avenged the blood of his servants at her
hand. 3 And again they said, Alleluia. And her smoke rose
up for ever and ever. 4 And the four and twenty elders and
the four beasts fell down and worshipped God that sat on
the throne, saying, Amen; Alleluia.

O for a thousand tongues to sing
My great Redeemers praise,
The glories of my God and king,
The triumphs of His grace!

My gracious master and my God,
Assist me to proclaim,

To spread through all the earth abroad
The honors of Thy name.

Jesus! the name that charms our fears,
That bids our sorrows cease;
Tis music in the sinners ears,
'Tis life, and health, and peace.

He breaks the power of canceled sin,
He sets the prisoner free;
His blood can make the foulest clean,
His blood availed for me.[1]

Small Saints and Great Saints Can Praise God

**5 And a voice came out of the throne, saying, Praise our
God, all ye his servants, and ye that fear him, both small
and great. 6 And I heard as it were the voice of a great
multitude, and as the voice of many waters, and as the
voice of mighty thunderings, saying, Alleluia: for the Lord
God omnipotent reigneth. 7 Let us be glad and rejoice, and
give honour to him: for the marriage of the Lamb is come,
and his wife hath made herself ready. 8 And to her was
granted that she should be arrayed in fine linen, clean and
white: for the fine linen is the righteousness of saints.**

While the Great Whore was clothed in sumptuous red and scarlet apparel, the Bride of Christ is clothed in fine linen, clean and white to symbolize the righteousness of the saints.

[1] Charles Wesley.

The Marriage Supper of the Lamb

[9] **And he saith unto me, Write, Blessed *are* they which are called unto the marriage supper of the Lamb. And he saith unto me, These are the true sayings of God.**

Improper Worship

[10] **And I fell at his feet to worship him. And he said unto me, See *thou do it* not: I am thy fellow servant, and of thy brethren that have the testimony of Jesus: worship God: for the testimony of Jesus is the spirit of prophecy.**

There is a fine line between showing respect, honor, and deference to a person, or being of an exalted rank, and bowing before them in an act of worship. In history, the Church has defended the use of icons in worship, in as far as only veneration was displayed. Formal worship was refused by Peter (Acts 10:25, 26), and by an angel (Rev. 22:8, 9). The word for worship (Gk. proskuneo) has the idea of bowing down or prostrating oneself in homage to show reverence. The angel said, "Do not bow down to me." By way of application, Christians should prayerfully consider the appropriateness of genuflecting, or kneeling in prayer before any image of God, Christ, a saint, or an angel.

Scene Ten: The Rider on a White Horse

[11] **And I saw heaven opened, and behold a white horse; and he that sat upon him *was* called Faithful and True, and in righteousness he doth judge and make war.**

One of the large and constant themes in Revelation is that the judgment of God on the wicked is righteous. God is always faithful to His own essence, He is true to His word, and His judgments are always righteous. As the righteous judge, the Lord cannot be bribed, He cannot be bought, He cannot be compromised.

12 His eyes *were* as a flame of fire, and on his head *were* many crowns; and he had a name written, that no man knew, but he himself.

The crowns which King Jesus wears are all the crowns of the universe, for all power has been given unto Him. The nations of earth are not without accountability. Every national leader is subject to the Sovereign Lord Jesus.

The idea of a hidden name has been noted before in Revelation. Upon reflection, the hidden name is not so hidden (Rev. 2:17; 19:12). The hidden name of Revelation 19:12 is said to be. The Word of God in verse 13. Elsewhere, John said, "The Word was made flesh" (John 1:14). And the angel said to Joseph, "thou shalt call his name Jesus" (Matt. 1:21). Every Christian knows the name of Jesus.

> There have been names that I have loved to hear,
>   But never has there been a name so dear
> To this heart of mine
>   As the name divine,
> The precious, precious name of Jesus.
>
> Jesus is the sweetest name I know,
>   And He's just the same as his holy name,
> And that's the reason why I love Him so;
>   Jesus is the sweetest name I know.

There is no name in earth or heaven above,
That we should give such honor and such love
As the blessed name
Let us all acclaim,
That wondrous, glorious name of Jesus.

And someday I shall see Him face to face
To thank and praise Him for His wondrous grace,
Which He gave to me, when He made me free,
The blessed Son of God called Jesus.[2]

**13 And he *was* clothed with a vesture dipped in blood:
and his name is called The Word of God. 14 And the armies
which were in heaven followed him upon white horses,
clothed in fine linen, white and clean. 15 And out of his
mouth goeth a sharp sword, that with it he should smite the nations: and he shall rule them with a rod of iron: and he treadeth the winepress of the fierceness and wrath of Almighty God.**

The message of Revelation is cyclical. The winepress of the wrath of God has been mentioned before (Rev. 14:19). The image is severe. When the Lord passes judgment on the wicked, they are crushed. Earlier in Revelation, Jesus was declared to be the Prince or Ruler of the kings of the earth (Rev. 1:5). That sovereignty is reaffirmed in this scene.

16 And he hath on *his* vesture and on his thigh a name written, KING OF KINGS, AND LORD OF LORDS.

---

[2] Lela B. Long.

Heavens Greatest Warrior
(Revelation 19:11–21)

- The Great Warrior rides a white horse.
- The Great Warrior is called Faithful and True.
- The Great Warrior judges in righteousness.
- The Great Warrior makes war.
- The Great Warrior has eyes as a flame of fire.
- The Great Warrior wears many crowns.
- The Great Warrior has a secret name.
- The Great Warrior is clothed with a vesture dipped in blood.
- The Great Warrior is called, The Word of God.
- The Great Warrior commands the armies which were in heaven which followed him upon white horses, clothed in fine linen, white and clean.
- The Great Warrior destroys with the power of His word.
- The Great Warrior rules with a rode of iron.
- The Great Warrior has a robe, and on His thigh is written, "KING OF KINGS, AND LORD OF LORDS."

Jesus as the Prince, or Ruler of all, Jesus as King of kings and Lord of lords, is not for the future. It is a present reality. Because of His power, because of His exaltation, because of His presence, there is no battle. The enemies of the Lord might assemble, but the Biblical image moves from an unholy gathering to an immediate triumph without a contest being waged against God Himself.

Scene Eleven: Death, Confinement, and Destruction

17 And I saw an angel standing in the sun; and he cried
with a loud voice, saying to all the fowls that fly in the

midst of heaven, Come and gather yourselves together unto the supper of the great God;

An allusion is made here to the image found in Ezekiel 39:17–23, setting forth the complete victory of God. The enemies of God are defeated; the spoils of war are to be enjoyed.

18 **That ye may eat the flesh of kings, and the flesh of captains, and the flesh of mighty men, and the flesh of horses, and of them that sit on them, and the flesh of all *men, both* free and bond, both small and great.**

As the Lord rewards both small and great who honor and fear Him (Rev. 11:19:5), He will harshly judge and destroy those who oppose Him, both small and great (Rev. 19:18). When the final books of God are opened, the small and great shall each be judged according to their works (Rev. 20:12). Those whose works are covered by Christ shall enjoy heaven. Those whose works are performed apart from Christ shall be cast into the Lake of Fire (Rev. 20:15).

An Unholy Gathering

19 **And I saw the beast, and the kings of the earth, and their armies, gathered together to make war against him that sat on the horse, and against his army.**

The Final Judgment on The Beast from the Sea, and the Beast from the Land (the False Prophet)

20 **And the beast was taken, and with him the false prophet that wrought miracles before him, with which he deceived them that had received the mark of the beast, and**

them that worshipped his image. These both were cast alive into a lake of fire burning with brimstone.

> Thus, it is in hell; they would die, but they cannot. The wicked shall be always dying but never dead; the smoke of the furnace ascends for ever and ever. Oh! who can endure thus to be ever upon the rack? This word "ever" breaks the heart. Wicked men do now think the Sabbaths long, and think a prayer long; but oh! how long will it be to lie in hell for ever and ever? (Thomas Watson)

21 **And the remnant were slain with the sword of him that sat upon the horse, which *sword* proceeded out of his mouth: and all the fowls were filled with their flesh.**

Once more there is a gathering for battle, but there is no battle. The Beast from the Sea was taken, along with the Beast from the Earth, who is the False Prophet, and both were cast in a Lake of Fire burning with brimstone.

Revelation Chapter 20

The Seventh Cycle

Scene Twelve: Judgment on the Dragon

1 **And I saw an angel come down from heaven, having the key of the bottomless pit and a great chain in his hand.**

A number of angels have paraded across the scenes in Revelation. At least fifty-one times angels have been part of the narrative. John has seen angels to the seven churches. He has seen a strong angel (Rev. 5:2), an angel with wings (Rev. 8:13), a mighty angel (Rev. 10:1), an angel with a loud voice (Rev. 14:9), and an angel standing in the sun (Rev. 19:17). Here, there is nothing special about this angel. This non-descript angel is dispatched by the Lord with the key of sovereign authority, and the chain of bondage to dispatch the Dragon who is unable to resist.

2 **And he laid hold on the dragon, that old serpent, which is the Devil, and Satan, and bound him a thousand years,**

Comprehensive Judgment

- Judgment on Babylon (Rev. 14:8)
- Judgment on mankind (Rev. 18:3, 9)
- Judgment on the Beast from the Sea (Rev. 19:20)
- Judgment on the Beast from the Land (False Prophet) (Rev. 19:20)
- Judgment on the Dragon (Rev. 20:1–3)
- Judgment on the Dead (Rev. 20:12–15)

The judgment of the Dragon speaks to the fact that the source of evil is judged. For this purpose, the Son of God was manifested, "that He might destroy the works of the devil" (1 John 3:8). In time, the Devil himself is to be destroyed, because he is the source for the evil the Beast from the Earth (False Prophet) does. He is behind the Beast from the Sea, which all the world wonders at. The Dragon, that Old Serpent, the Devil is behind the fall of man, and the rebellion of the angels in heaven. It was the Devil who said he would be like the Most High. It was the Devil who said he would be exalted. His judgment is just. He is bound "a thousand years."

This is the only time in the Bible the thousand years, the millennial, is mentioned. In six verses it is mentioned seven times.

The Millennial of Revelation 20

- The millennial is when Satan is bound (Rev. 20:2)
- The millennial is when the nations are no longer deceived (Rev. 20:3).
- The millennial is when the saints reign with Jesus (Rev. 20:4).
- The millennial is the first resurrection (Rev. 20:5).

- The millennial is when priests reign with Christ (Rev. 20:6).
- The millennial is designed to expire (Rev. 20:7).

Though the millennial is spoken of so little in Scripture, it is spoken about a great deal in the Church, and in secular society. In the Church there are theological constructs. There is the Premillennial position, that argues Christ will return *before* the millennial. There is the Postmillennial position, that says Christ will return visibly *after* the millennial. There is the Amillennial position, that says the millennial is a present reality with a fuller manifestation at the Second Advent.

There are a number of reasons why there is great interest in the millennial, not the least of which is the fertile imaginations of men to exploit, and sensationalize a passage of Scripture.

In context, what might have been a sensational moment for those who heard Revelation initially read, was the length of time given to the binding of the Dragon, that Ancient Serpent, who is the Devil, and Satan. Up to this point in Revelation, the time periods have been relatively short: ten days, a half hour, one hour, five months, forty-two months, or three- and one-half years. Suddenly there is a thousand-year time period.

The time surprise is compounded when it is remembered that Revelation begins and ends by saying the events will happen soon (Rev. 1:1; 22:6). The time is short. That is the great message of Revelation, except for here. How is it possible for the judgment on the Devil to take so long?

Part of the answer is found in the various events that are scheduled to happen during the thousand years.

An Opportunity for Evangelism

3 And cast him into the bottomless pit, and shut him up, and set a seal upon him, that he should deceive the nations no more, till the thousand years should be fulfilled: and after that he must be loosed a little season.

The Dragon of Revelation 20 is to be contrasted with the Dragon of Revelation 12. The personage is the same, but his power is not. In one part of his existence, the Dragon, the Old Serpent, the Devil, who is Satan, is given freedom by God to portray himself as a Trinity with great power, to the point that he can persuade those who dwell on the earth to worship him by way of idolatry. Time passes, and God judges the earth. God judges nations in general, and mankind in particular. God judges every expression of evil, reflected in the Beast from the Sea, and the Beast from the Land being imprisoned. Then, God judges evil itself in the Father of all lies, the Dragon.

Remember that, in Revelation 12, the Church is faithful, and refused to receive the mark of the beast, or to worship his form. In Revelation 20, the Church is triumphant and the Dragon is put in prison. His power is diminished.

What a wonderful overview of history was given to the Churches of Asia in the first century. God's people were told that while the Church was weak, and it was, and the Dragon was strong, and he was, the time would come when the Church would be strong, and the Dragon would be weak, and imprisoned. The spiritual table would be turned. The principle of sowing and reaping would be confirmed. Those who sowed to the flesh by following the Dragon, and his two Beasts, would reap death and damnation. No matter how dark Church history may become, there is hope for the future. That is the Big Picture of Revelation.

There is another message the Church in the first century, and the Church in every generation can apply. It is the Focused Picture.

From one perspective, in every era of the existence of the Church, she is both weak and strong. A. W. Tozer talked about the Christian paradoxes.

> A real Christian is an odd number anyway. He feels supreme love for One whom he has never seen, talks familiarly every day to Someone he cannot see, expects to go to heaven on the virtue of Another, empties himself in order to be full, admits he is wrong so he can be declared right, goes down in order to get up, is strongest when he is weakest, richest when he is poorest, and happiest when he feels worst. He dies so he can live, forsakes in order to have, gives away so he can keep, sees the invisible, hears the inaudible, and knows that which passeth knowledge.[1]

From another perspective, the Dragon is both strong and weak, in every generation, of every era in Church history, until the Lord returns. Because the Dragon is strong, he can work wonders and draw the hearts of men after himself, or those he controls. Because the Dragon is weak, he is contained and restrained by the power of God.

Evidence for the weakness of the Dragon abounds as much as evidence of his power. For example, the Devil cannot deceive the nations, at this time, which is why worldwide evange-

[1] A. W. Tozer. *The Root of Righteousness* (Chicago, IL: Moody, 2015), 189.

lism can take place. The Devil cannot destroy the Church, no matter how hard he tries, and in all the ways he makes that effort. The Gates of Hell shall never prevail against the Church. Why? Because Satan is contained, and restrained.

When the Church is sufferring, and feels oppressed by the world, the flesh, and the Devil, the comfort of God's Word comes to say, "The time is short." When the Devil comes to try to deceive Christians, the Word of God says the Lord will preserve, and protect His people.

As there is the Big Picture of Revelation 20, and the Focused Picture, so there is the Practical Picture.

The binding of Satan becomes an encouragement to the Church to continue to do what Christ has commanded the Church to do, and that is to make disciples in all nations. How is that possible? Because there is plenty of time. That is the importance of the thousand years. God is going to give to the Church enough time to accomplish His will of bringing the gospel to every tongue, and nation, and tribe. While there is always a sense of urgency associated with the work of the Lord, there is also the assurance that God will make sure there is enough time to accomplish His will. Noah was given 120 years to build the Ark, because God knew that much time was needed. The Church needs a thousand years to advance the gospel, and that much time will be given it, at the very least.

Then, the text says, the Dragon will be released for "a little season" (Gk. *mikros*; small), a micro, or extremely little amount of time. According to Merriam-Webster, microtime is "a very short interval of time (as 0.01 millionth of a second)." The phrase, "a little season" (*mikros*), is used one other time in the vision, Revelation 6:11, to underscore the shortness of time.

There is another possible understanding of the phrase, "a little season." With the understanding that, in Revelation, sequence does not always mean chronology, the little season takes place "amid" (Gk. *meta*), the thousand-year reign.

Without being dogmatic, Church historian, Dr. Robert Godfrey, postulates this possibility. It is an idea worth considering. "What John is saying here is that there is the thousand years, and there is the 'little time,' and they are the same."

One reason to consider the "little season" coinciding with the millennial is this: "How can Jesus come as a thief in the night if there is an intensification of demonic activity prior to his Advent?"

Jesus did say the wheat and the tares would grow together. "Let both grow together until the harvest: and in the time of harvest I will say to the reapers, Gather ye together first the tares, and bind them in bundles to burn them: but gather the wheat into my barn" (Matt. 13:30).

Jesus did teach that life would be normal prior to His return. "For as in the days that were before the flood they were eating and drinking, marrying and giving in marriage, until the day that Noe entered into the ark, And knew not until the flood came, and took them all away; so shall also the coming of the Son of man be" (Matt. 24:38–39).

The time the Church needs to fulfill the Great Commission is but a little season for Satan to work. Indeed, the Devil knows his time is short (Rev. 12:12).

Judgment by the Martyred Saints

4 And I saw thrones, and they sat upon them, and judgment was given unto them: and *I saw* the souls of them that were beheaded for the witness of Jesus, and for the word of God, and which had not worshipped the beast, neither his image, neither had received *his* mark upon their foreheads, or in their hands; and they lived and reigned with Christ a thousand years.

It is an incredible scene John beholds. The souls that were beheaded lived. They came to life, and that is not death. The martyred saints lived, as do all who die in Christ, and they reigned with him a thousand years. This is not something John witnessed for the far distinct future. This was a present reality to him, as it should be to the Church in every generation. God's people need comfort when they are dying, and when a funeral service takes place. What better message than to know that death is not the termination of everything, but the exaltation of the believer. To be away from home in the body, is to be at home with the Lord. To be at home with the Lord is to live. It is to be an overcomer. It is to reign with Him in glory, not on the earth. The thrones are in heaven. The souls that live are in heaven. Those who reign with Christ a thousand years do so in heaven.

The judges who occupy the thrones are the souls of those martyred for being a faithful witness for Jesus. Their lives had been poured out like sacrificial blood "under the altar" (Rev. 6:9-11). They died in the Lord (Rev. 14:13).

The First Resurrection

[5] But the rest of the dead lived not again until the thousand years were finished. This *is* the first resurrection.

The "rest of the dead" refers to the wicked. The ungodly are not unconscious. Jesus made that clear in His story of Lazarus and the rich man in hell. However, the "rest of the dead," those who are outside of Christ, have no quality to their dark and painful existence. It is the coming to life in Christ which is the first resurrection. Paul spoke about this spiritual resurrection in Ephesians 2:1, 6. "And you hath he quickened, who were dead in trespasses and sins . . . And hath raised us up together, and made us sit together in heavenly places in Christ Jesus."

The words of Paul, and the words of John, are identical. The dead come to life, are raised, and enthroned in heaven to share Christ's royal reign. Neither describe the believer's future bodily resurrection, ascension, and enthronement, because the spiritual reality is in the present. Grace is received by faith, which is a gift of God (Eph. 2:8). The resurrection life of Christ and His heavenly reign is presently shared. "If ye then be risen with Christ, seek those things which are above, where Christ sitteth on the right hand of God. Set your affection on things above, not on things on the earth. For ye are dead, and your life is hid with Christ in God. When Christ, who is our life, shall appear, then shall ye also appear with him in glory" (Col. 3:1–4).

Jesus spoke of the first resurrection in John 5:25 saying, "Verily, verily, I say unto you, The hour is coming, and now is, when the dead shall hear the voice of the Son of God: and they that hear shall live." When a person effectually hears the voice of Jesus, they live.

6 Blessed and holy *is* he that hath part in the first resurrection: on such the second death hath no power, but they shall be priests of God and of Christ, and shall reign with him a thousand years.

The second death is at the final judgment. What an awful death that shall be. In contrast, the spiritual reality is that those who have died in the Lord are the priests of God and shall reign with Him a thousand (Gk. *chilioi*; plural of uncertain affinity) years. The promise could be stated that the priests of God shall reign with Christ for thousands of years, reaffirming the concept that the Church will be given enough time to complete the work assigned to her by Jesus in Matthew 28:18-20. In one sense, there is no need to be unduly anxious about the work of evangelism, though we are to work diligently until the Lord comes.

Scene Thirteen: A Final Deception for a Micro Second

7 And when the thousand years are expired, Satan shall be loosed out of his prison, 8 And shall go out to deceive the nations which are in the four quarters of the earth, Gog and Magog, to gather them together to battle: the number of whom *is* as the sand of the sea.

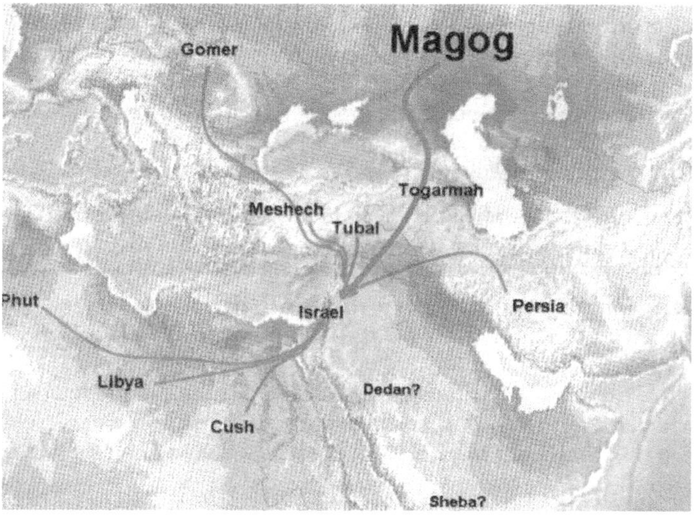

Historically, Gog, from the land of Magog, was the leader of a confederacy of armies that marched from the north against Israel. The prophet Ezekiel wrote about Gog. "And the word of the Lord came unto me, saying, Son of man, set thy face against Gog, the land of Magog, the chief prince of Meshech and Tubal, and prophesy against him . . . Thus will I magnify myself, and sanctify myself; and I will be known in the eyes of many nations, and they shall know that I am the Lord" (Ezek. 38:1, 2, 23).

Alluding to ancient events, John sees that the glory of God will once again be manifested in the final judgment to come.

To take God and Magog and superimpose a modern-day nation into the text in order to advance an eschatological bias would be to violate the proper understanding of the passage. There is a message here for God's people in every generation. The message is this: The time will come when all the enemies of the Lord, and His anointed, are gathered and destroyed. Though the enemies of God gather as "the sand of the sea," it does not matter. God also has an elect people whose number is as "the stars of the heaven, and as the sand which is upon the sea shore" (Gen. 22:17). It is the seed of the Lord that shall possess the gate of their enemies because God will devour every enemy of the Church.

9 **And they went up on the breadth of the earth, and compassed the camp of the saints about, and the beloved city: and fire came down from God out of heaven, and devoured them.**

In the ancient vision Ezekiel saw, Gog was to be crushed on the mountains of Israel. The slaughter was to be so vast, seven months would be necessary to bury the dead. "And seven months shall the house of Israel be burying of them, that they may cleanse the land" (Ezek. 39:12).

In the final judgment which John saw, the enemies of God, numbering like the sand of the seas, will be crushed by the glory of the Lord, His power, majesty, and might. The saints of the Lord will be protected. The unrighteous will be devoured. And best of all, there will be no battle, though the ungodly are gathered, because fire comes down from God. The war is over before any battle is engaged. "*Our God reigns!*"

The End of the Leaders of the Pack

10 **And the devil that deceived them was cast into the lake of fire and brimstone, where the beast and the false prophet *are*, and shall be tormented day and night for ever and ever.**

Those who lead individuals into rebellion, sin, idolatry, and immoral acts shall be destroyed. The Dragon, who is called that Old Serpent, the Devil, shall be cast into the Lake of Fire.

The Beast from the Sea, and the Beast from the Earth, which is the False Prophet, shall be tormented with the Devil day and night forever and ever. If a headstone were to be made for the Devil, the epitaph would read as follows: "HE WAS STRONG. HE WAS WEAK. HE WAS DESTROYED."

Let Him that have ears to hear, hear what the Spirit says to the Church. Receiving the blessing of faith.

Scene Fourteen: The Great White Throne Judgment

11 And I saw a great white throne, and him that sat on it, from whose face the earth and the heaven fled away; and there was found no place for them. 12 And I saw the dead, small and great, stand before God; and the books were opened: and another book was opened, which is *the book* of life: and the dead were judged out of those things which were written in the books, according to their works.

The teaching of the Church has always been that each person will give an account to God for the life they have lived. "For we must all appear before the judgment seat of Christ; that everyone may receive the things done in his body, according to that he hath done, whether it be good or bad" (2 Cor. 5:10).

As God judges the angels, good and bad, as God judged Adam, the Federal Representative of the Human Race, as God judged His own Son, Jesus Christ, as God judged the Dragon, and the two Beasts, so God will judge all mankind, small and great. The basis of judgment will be the books; "the books were opened."

There is the Book of Life. This is the book in which the Saviour writes the names of the elect whom He has redeemed before the foundation of the world (Eph. 1:4).

There are other books, in which are written the deeds of individuals, who have demanded to be judged according to their works. No one should every want to be judged out of the books of deeds because they will be weighted in the balances, and found wanting, as short of righteousness, as King Belshazzar (Dan. 5:27).

13 **And the sea gave up the dead which were in it; and death and hell delivered up the dead which were in them: and they were judged every man according to their works.**

There will be a bodily resurrection of those who have died physically. While it is not labeled, this is the "second resurrection" implied in the "first resurrection" of Revelation 20:6.

Scene Fifteen: Eternal Judgment: The Second Death

14 **And death and hell [hades] were cast into the lake of fire [*gehenna*]. This is the second death.** 15 **And whosoever was not found written in the book of life was cast into the lake of fire.**

Whatever the nature of hell (*gehenna*) is, in its final expression, it is a terrible place, a place to which Jesus warned no one wants to go. Jesus also declared that it would have been better had Judas never been born than to face the consequences of his actions in hell (Mark 14:16). It is a place of everlasting destruction (2 Thess. 1:9). The Puritan Thomas Watson said, "The torments of hell abide for ever. If all the earth and sea were sand, and every thousandth year a bird should come, and take away one grain of this sand, it would be a long time ere that vast heap of sand were emptied; yet, if after all that time the damned may come out of hell, there were some hope; but this word ever breaks the heart."[2]

[2] Thomas Watson. *A Body of Practical Divinity* (Philadelphia, PA: James Kay, 1840), 240.

Revelation Chapter 21

The Seventh Cycle

Scene Sixteen: A New Heaven and a New Earth

[1] **And I saw a new heaven and a new earth: for the first heaven and the first earth were passed away; and there was no more sea.**

The new world John sees is a world that is stable, and without threat or separation. The sea separated John from those he loved so much. They were on the mainland in Asia, he was on the isle of Patmos. The time will come when loved ones will never be separated again.

[2] **And I John saw the holy city, new Jerusalem, coming down from God out of heaven, prepared as a bride adorned for her husband.**

In a happy mixture of metaphors, John sees the Holy City, New Jerusalem, descending from heaven, and it brings to the mind of John, a beautiful bride.

Images of the Church

Christ	Church	
• Vine	Branches	John 15:5
• Shepherd	Sheep	John 10:1–18
• High Priest	Believer priests	1 Pet. 2:9
• Head	Body	Col. 1:18; 1 Cor. 12:27
• Light	Lampstand	John 9:5; Rev. 2:1
• King	A Holy Nation	1 Tim. 1:17–20; 1 Pet. 2:9
• Bridegroom	Bride	Eph. 5:32
• Chief Cornerstone	Foundation	Eph. 2:20

For most of Revelation, John has witnessed a dramatic distinction between heaven and earth. Heaven is a lovely place. There is a Heavenly Temple. Holy angels are in heaven who praise God, and serve Him day and night. The Martyred Saints are in heaven. There are thrones in heaven. On the thrones sit the twenty-four elders. Circling the throne are four living creatures. Songs are sung in heaven. It is a place of grandeur, wonder, and fascination.

Heaven is contrasted throughout Revelation with tumultuous events on earth. The Four Horsemen ride, bringing conquest, war, famine, pestilence, and death. There is much death and destruction. The Beast from the Sea arises, and the Beast from the Earth comes to be energized and controlled by the Dragon. Judgment falls on Mystery Babylon. War is made on the saints. The universe is in turmoil. Suddenly, all is calm and peaceful. There is a new heaven, and a new earth. There is a beautiful city descending to earth, an earth on which there is no more sea. Heaven comes to earth.

If anyone wants a preview of the glory that is to come, believe on the Lord Jesus Christ, and you will know something of heaven coming down.

O what a wonderful, wonderful day—Day I will never forget;
After I'd wandered in darkness away, Jesus my Savior I met.
O what a tender, compassionate Friend—
He met the need of my heart;
Shadows dispelling, with joy I am telling,
He made all the darkness depart.

Heaven came down and glory filled my soul,
When at the cross the Saviour made me whole;
My sins were washed away—And my night was turned to day—
Heaven came down and glory filled my soul!

Born of the Spirit with life from above into God's family divine,
Justified fully thru Calvary's love, O what a standing is mine!
And the transaction so quickly was made when as a sinner I came,
Took of the offer of grace He did proffer—He saved me, O praise His dear name!

Now I've a hope that will surely endure after the passing of time;
I have a future in heaven for sure, there in those mansions sublime.
And its because of that wonderful day, when at the cross I believed;

Riches eternal and blessings supernal, from His precious
hand I
received.

Heaven came down and glory filled my soul,
When at the cross the Saviour made me whole;
My sins were washed away—
And my night was turned to day—
Heaven came down and glory filled my soul!
Heaven came down and glory filled my soul!

An Eternal Covenant with God

3 And I heard a great voice out of heaven saying, Behold, the tabernacle of God *is* with men, and he will dwell with them, and they shall be his people, and God himself shall be with them, *and be* their God.

One of the most comforting truths in the Bible is that God is a covenant keeping God. He will tabernacle, or dwell with His people, and be their God. "Know therefore that the Lord thy God, he is God, the faithful God, which keepeth covenant and mercy with them that love him and keep his commandments to a thousand generations" (Deut. 7:9).

"The everlasting covenant which God has made with Jesus, and through Jesus with all His beloved people, individually, is a strong ground of consolation amidst the tremblings of human hope, the fluctuations of creature things, and the instability of what earth calls good" (Octavius Winslow). Let the Church believe God when He says, "I will never break my covenant with you" (Jdgs. 2:1).

4 And God shall wipe away all tears from their eyes; and there shall be no more death, neither sorrow, nor crying, neither shall there be any more pain: for the former things are passed away.

When God dwells with His people, He comforts them in their sorrow, and takes away their pain. In time, the former things are passed away, to include sin, sickness, hunger, death, and the terrors of life. The former things are passed away, because, "God is so generous that He gives us grace that we do not deserve, love that we cannot comprehend, and mercy that we cannot resist" (Unknown).

Among the former things to pass away, is sin. In the fall of humanity, man became guilty before God, corrupt in nature, and spiritually dead. Christ came to remove the guilt, create a new nature, and regenerate the soul. In the glory that shall come, there will be no more guilt, no more corruption, and no more death, all of which brings misery to the heart, and tears to the eyes.

5 And he that sat upon the throne said, Behold, I make all things new. And he said unto me, Write: for these
words are true and faithful. 6 And he said unto me, It is done. I am Alpha and Omega, the beginning and the end. I will give unto him that is athirst of the fountain of the water of life freely.

When God begins to bring a soul to Himself, a spiritual thirst is created. Jesus said, "Blessed are they which do hunger and thirst after righteousness: for they shall be filled" (Matt. 5:6). Jesus is the fountain of life. "In the last day, that great day of the feast, Jesus stood and cried, saying, If any man thirst, let him come unto me, and drink. He that believeth on me, as the scripture hath said, out of his belly shall flow rivers of living water" (John 7:37–38). "As the hart panteth after the water brooks, so panteth my soul after thee, O God" (Ps. 42:1).

Some of the people in Athens were thirsty, but they tried to quench their spiritual thirst by worshipping idols. Paul took notice, and said to the people from Mars Hill, "I perceive that in all things you are more religious than others" (Acts 17:22). Paul preached Christ to the Athenians. "And when they heard of the resurrection of the dead, some mocked: and others said, We will hear thee again of this matter" (Acts 17:32).

There was a man from Ethiopia who was thirsty. In the providence of God, he met Philip who preached unto him Jesus (Acts 8:36). The Ethiopian found his spiritual thirst satisfied by the gospel.

One night a ruler of the Jews came to Jesus. His name was Nicodemus, and he was spiritually thirsty. He wanted to know the way of salvation, and was told he had to be born again. Nicodemus was born from above, and his spiritual thirst was quenched (John 3:1–16).

7 **He that overcometh shall inherit all things; and I will be his God, and he shall be my son.** 8 **But the fearful, and unbelieving, and the abominable, and murderers, and whoremongers, and sorcerers, and idolaters, and all liars, shall have their part in the lake which burneth with fire and brimstone: which is the second death.**

There are sins which will disqualify a person from being a child of God. God will not be the God of certain individuals, in a personal and intimate way, apart from gospel repentance (1 Cor. 6:11). They are listed in Scripture.

This particular list of the damned begins with cowards. A person who is a coward will not persevere in the Christian faith in times of persecution, or testing. "Demas hath forsaken me," wrote Paul with sadness, "having loved this present world, and is departed unto Thessalonica" (2 Tim. 4:10). John remembered how he had written in his gospel about certain individuals. They were fearful. They were cowards. They were faithless. "From that time many of his disciples went back, and walked no more with him" (John 6:66).

Those Among the Damned
Sin in the Sanctuaries

- The fearful: Gk. *deilos*; timid, i.e. (by implication) faithless SARDIS
- The unbelieving: Gk. *apistos*; disbelieving, i.e. without Christian faith SMYRNA
- The abominable: Gk. *bdelusso*; to be disgusted, i.e. (by implication) detest SMYRNA
- Murderers: Gk. *phoneus*; a criminal murderer PERGAMUM
- Whoremongers: Gk. *pornos*; a (male) prostitute; a libertine THYATIRA
- Sorcerers: Gk. *pharmakeus*; a druggist; poisoner; a magician LAODICEA
- Idolaters: Gk. *eidololatres*; an image servant or worshipper PERGAMOS
- Liars: Gk. *pseudoes*; untrue, i.e. erroneous, deceitful, wicked EPHESUS

Christ calls the Church to consider who the people of God really are. They are invited to drink from the river of life. All others are warned.

Rise up, O men of God!
Have done with lesser things.
Give heart and mind and soul and strength
To serve the King of kings.[1]

The Ending of the Cycle: A Picture of the Bride of Christ: The Last Great Woman: The Church

9 And there came unto me one of the seven angels which had the seven vials full of the seven last plagues, and talked with me, saying, Come hither, I will shew thee the bride, the Lamb's Wife.

Four times in Revelation the words, "Come hither" are used. First, John was told to "come hither," and be shown things which were to be hereafter his initial view of the resurrected Christ (Rev 4:1). Second, the Two Witnesses, Moses and Elijah, were told to "come up hither", as they were removed to heaven in a cloud while their enemies watched (Rev 11:12). Third, John was told to "come hither" in order to see the judgment of the Great Whore (Rev 17:1). Fourth, John was told to "come hither" in order to be shown the bride, the Lamb's wife (Rev 21:9).

It must not be missed that the Lamb's Wife is the Great City. The Holy Jerusalem is the Bride of Christ. Those who press for a literal city, meeting the precise description of what John saw, will miss the majesty and glory of the imagery. In a quest for an external object, the Church will not hear what the Bridegroom is saying about His Bride. In prosaic language, John is being shown what the Lord thinks of His wife. She is

---

[1] William H. Walter.

altogether lovely. She is glorious! "This is my beloved, and this is my friend, O daughters of Jerusalem" (Song 5:16).

**10 And he carried me away in the spirit to a great and
high mountain, and shewed me that great city, the holy
Jerusalem, descending out of heaven from God, 11 Having
the glory of God: and her light *was* like unto a stone most
precious, even like a jasper stone, clear as crystal; 12 And
had a wall great and high, *and* had twelve gates, and at the
gates twelve angels, and names written thereon, which are
the names of the twelve tribes of the children of Israel: 13
On the east three gates; on the north three gates; on the
south three gates; and on the west three gates. 14 And the
wall of the city had twelve foundations, and in them the
names of the twelve apostles of the Lamb.**

In the image of the Lamb's Wife, the Holy City, the New Jerusalem, are united all the true children of Israel, those who have the faith of Abraham, Isaac, and Jacob.

In the image of the Lamb's Wife are united all those represented by the twelve apostles. The saints of the Old Testament, and the saints of the New Covenant are one in the Lamb's Wife and she is One with the Lamb as Bridegroom.

There is a beautiful mixture of images, and conflating of ideas, in order to convey something beyond human ability to articulate.

All that Christ is, all that the Church is meant to be, flows into a final event, which fulfills the promise whereby Christ presents to Himself a glorious Church, "not having spot, or wrinkle, or any such thing; but that it should be holy and without blemish" (Eph. 5:26).

[15] And he that talked with me had a golden reed to
measure the city, and the gates thereof, and the wall thereof. [16] And the city lieth foursquare, and the length is as
large as the breadth: and he measured the city with the
reed, twelve thousand furlongs. The length and the
breadth and the height of it are equal. [17] And he measured
the wall thereof, an hundred *and* forty *and* four cubits, *according to* the measure of a man, that is, of the angel. [18]
And the building of the wall of it was *of* jasper: and the
city *was* pure gold, like unto clear glass. [19] And the foundations of the wall of the city *were* garnished with all manner
of precious stones. The first foundation *was* jasper; the
second, sapphire; the third, a chalcedony; the fourth, an
emerald; [20] The fifth, sardonyx; the sixth, sardius; the seventh, chrysolite; the eighth, beryl; the ninth, a topaz; the
tenth, a chrysoprasus; the eleventh, a jacinth; the twelfth,
an amethyst. [21] And the twelve gates *were* twelve pearls;
every several gate was of one pearl: and the street of the
city *was* pure gold, as it were transparent glass. [22] And I
saw no temple therein: for the Lord God Almighty and the
Lamb are the temple of it. [23] And the city had no need of
the sun, neither of the moon, to shine in it: for the glory
of God did lighten it, and the Lamb *is* the light thereof. [24]
And the nations of them which are saved shall walk in the
light of it: and the kings of the earth do bring their glory
and honour into it. [25] And the gates of it shall not be shut
at all by day: for there shall be no night there. [26] And they
shall bring the glory and honour of the nations into it. [27]
And there shall in no wise enter into it any thing that de-

fileth, neither *whatsoever* worketh abomination, or *maketh* a lie: but they which are written in the Lamb's book of life.

Characteristics of the Holy City

- The city is a prepared city, for a prepared people. (v. 2)
- The city comes down from God as His unique creation. (v. 2)
- The city is the Tabernacle of God with men. (v. 3)
- The city is a place of happiness. (v. 4)
- The city is free of every form of wickedness. (v. 8)
- The city is the Lamb's Wife. (vv. 9, 10)
- The city has the glory of God as her essence. (v. 11)
- The city embraces all the faithful children of Israel. (v. 12)
- The city embraces those built on the apostles of the Lamb. (v. 13)
- The city, when measured, is large, and perfectly designed. (vv. 15–18)
- The city is lavished with priceless jewels. (vv. 19–21)
- The city has no Temple, nothing to distance people from God. (v. 22)
- The city has no artificial light. (v. 23)
- The city is the place of worship for all nations. (v. 24; cf. Ps. 138:4, 5)
- The city is free, and open to all, for it is safe. (v. 25)
- The city is holy. (v. 27)

The church's one Foundation
  is Jesus Christ her Lord;
she is His new creation,
  by water and the Word;
from heav'n He came and sought her
  to be His holy bride;

with His own blood He bought her,
    and for her life He died.

Elect from evr'y nation,
    yet one o'er all the earth,
her charter of salvation,
    one Lord, one faith, one birth;
one holy Name she blesses,
    partakes one holy food,
and to one hope she presses,
    with evr'y grace endued.

The church shall never perish!
    Her dear Lord, to defend,
to guide, sustain, and cherish,
    is with her to the end;
tho' there be those that hate her
    and false sons in her pale,
against the foe or traitor
    she ever shall prevail.

Mid toil and tribulation,
    and tumult of her war,
she waits the consummation
    of peace for evermore;
till with the vision glorious
    her longing eyes are blest,
and the great church victorious
    shall be the church at rest.[2]

---

[2] Samuel John Stone.

Revelation Chapter 22

[1] **And he showed me a pure river of water of life, clear as crystal, proceeding out of the throne of God and of the Lamb.**

In a dry and arid land, water is greatly valued. In the eternal state, there is a river of precious water, and an abundance of food to enjoy. There is no more scarcity of water or food.

[2] **In the midst of the street of it, and on either side of the river, *was there* the tree of life, which bare twelve *manner* of fruits, *and* yielded her fruit every month: and the leaves of the tree *were* for the healing of the nations.**

The prophet Ezekiel had seen something very similar in his vision. "And by the river upon the bank thereof, on this side and on that side, shall grow all trees for meat, whose leaf shall not fade, neither shall the fruit thereof be consumed: it shall bring forth new fruit according to his months, because their waters they issued out of the sanctuary: and the fruit thereof shall be for meat, and the leaf thereof for medicine" (Ezek. 47:12).

The Psalmist said, "The righteous shall flourish like the palm tree: he shall grow like a cedar in Lebanon. Those that be planted in the house of the Lord shall flourish in the courts of our God. They shall still bring forth fruit in old age; they shall be fat and flourishing; To shew that the Lord is upright: he is my rock, and there is no unrighteousness in him" (Psalm 92:12–15).

In the Bible, a tree symbolizes life, fruitfulness, and healing. Is it any wonder that John sees the Tree of Life in the new heaven and the new earth?

3 **And there shall be no more curse: but the throne of God and of the Lamb shall be in it; and his servants shall serve him:**
4 **And they shall see his face; and his name *shall be* in their foreheads.**

Face to face with Christ, my Savior,
  Face to face—what will it be,
When with rapture I behold Him,
  Jesus Christ who died for me?

Face to face I shall behold Him,
  Far beyond the starry sky;
Face to face in all His glory,
  I shall see Him by and by!

Only faintly now I see Him,
  With the darkened veil between,
But a blessed day is coming,
  When His glory shall be seen.
What rejoicing in His presence,
  When are banished grief and pain;
When the crooked ways are straightened,
  And the dark things shall be plain.

Face to face—oh, blissful moment!
  Face to face—to see and know;

Face to face with my Redeemer,
Jesus Christ who loves me so.[1]

[5] And there shall be no night there; and they need no candle, neither light of the sun; for the Lord God giveth them light: and they shall reign for ever and ever.

The eternal blessing of the saints is set in contrast to those who are cast into "the Lake which burneth with fire and brimstone: which is the second death" (Rev. 20:15). The prophet has looked forward to the day when heaven will open and the Bride of Christ will be on display to be united with the Lamb forever. The Church will linger near a pure river of life, and enjoy twelve manner of fruits whose leaves are for the healing of the nations (Ezek. 47:12). The saints shall serve the Lamb for all eternity, and with a sweet spirit. Best of all, the redeemed shall see Jesus face to face, and His name shall be forever in their foreheads.

Conclusion: A Promise and a Blessing

[6] And he said unto me, These sayings *are* faithful and true: and the Lord God of the holy prophets sent his angel to shew unto his servants the things which must shortly be done. [7] Behold, I come quickly: blessed is he that keepeth the sayings of the prophecy of this book. [8] And I John saw these things, and heard *them*. And when I had heard and seen, I fell down to worship before the feet of the angel which shewed me these things. [9] Then saith he unto me, See *thou do it* not: for I am thy fellow servant, and of thy

[1] Carrie E. Breck.

brethren the prophets, and of them which keep the sayings of this book: worship God. [10] And he saith unto me, Seal not the sayings of the prophecy of this book: for the time is at hand.

Daniel was told to seal up his vison, while John is specifically told not to seal the sayings of the prophecy of this book (Dan. 8:26; 12:4). Why? Because "the time is at hand." Here is some good news. There is nothing more that needs to be done as far as prophecy is concerned other than to wait patiently for the Lord's return. At the Second Advent, there will be a final gathering and separating of the saved from the lost. When Jesus comes there will be a general resurrection of the dead. There will be a final judgment. There will be a renovation of the universe. It shall be rolled up like a scroll and unrolled again to form a new heaven and a new earth where in dwells righteousness. Never again will sin be allowed to mar God's creation, for all things are made new.

[11] He that is unjust, let him be unjust still: and he which is filthy, let him be filthy still: and he that is righteous, let him be righteous still: and he that is holy, let him be holy still.

In the Revelation, people rarely change sides, if ever. There is an "us" against "them" concept that prevails the narrative. The unjust remain unjust. Those who are morally and spiritually filthy remain filthy. Those who are righteous are righteous still. Those who are holy and set apart are holy still. The reason for this entrenchment, in part, is because the emphasis is on encouraging the saints to be faithful, persevere, and conquer.

[12] And, behold, I come quickly; and my reward *is* with me, to give every man according as his work shall be. [13] I

**am Alpha and Omega, the beginning and the end, the first
and the last. 14 Blessed *are* they that do his commandments, that they may have right to the tree of life, and may
enter in through the gates into the city. 15 For without *are*
dogs, and sorcerers, and whoremongers, and murderers,
and idolaters, and whosoever loveth and maketh a lie. 16 I
Jesus have sent mine angel to testify unto you these things
in the churches. I am the root and the offspring of David,
and the bright and morning star.**

The Great Gospel Invitation

17 And the Spirit and the bride say, Come. And let him that heareth say, Come. And let him that is athirst come. And whosoever will, let him take the water of life freely.

Together the Holy Spirit and the Church unite to say to the world, "Come! Come to Jesus! Come to the Marriage Supper of the Lamb! Come to the New Jerusalem! Come!" The Church must evangelize. There is a sense of urgency associated with evangelism. "Behold now is the accepted time; behold, now is the day of salvation" (2 Cor. 6:2).

> Come, ye sinners, poor and needy,
>   Weak and wounded, sick and sore!
> Jesus ready stands to save you,
>   Full of pity, love and power.
> He is able, He is able, He is able,
>   He is willing, doubt no more!
>
> Let not conscience let you linger,
>   Nor of fitness fondly dream;

All the fitness he requireth
    Is to feel your need of him.
This he gives you,
    This he gives you, This he gives you:
Tis the Spirits glimmering beam.

Come ye weary, heavy laden,
    Bruised and mangled by the fall;
If you tarry till you're better,
    You will never come at all.
Not the righteous, Not the righteous, Not the righteous;
    Sinners Jesus came to call.

A Serious Warning

18 For I testify unto every man that heareth the words of the prophecy of this book, If any man shall add unto these things, God shall add unto him the plagues that are written in this book: 19 And if any man shall take away from the words of the book of this prophecy, God shall take away his part out of the book of life, and out of the holy city, and *from* the things which are written in this book.

When God made His covenant with Israel, the people were warned not to take anything away from it, or add to the covenant. "Ye shall not add unto the word which I command you, neither shall ye diminish ought from it, that ye may keep the commandments of the LORD your God which I command you" (Deut. 4:2). When God made the New Covenant, the principle remained.

Throughout time the temptation has come to diminish the Word of God, substitute its teachings, or add to it. The Book of Mormon boldly proclaims to be equal to the Bible. The Introduction to the volume declares, "The Book of Mormon is a volume of holy scripture comparable to the Bible." Many Seventh-day Adventist view Ellen G. White as an inspired prophetess of God. Therefore, her writings are to be placed along side of Scripture. The same is true for many who follow the teachings of Christian Science as set forth by Mary Baker Eddy in Science and Health with Key to the Scriptures. By adding to the Bible, these religious leaders, and their followers, are in violation of God's will.

A Promise, A Prayer, and a Blessing

20 He which testifieth these things saith, Surely I come quickly. Amen. Even so, come, Lord Jesus.

The Revelation opened with the promise of events that would "shortly come to pass" (Rev. 1:1). The Revelation closes with the promise that Jesus is coming "quickly" (Gk. *tachu*; shortly, i.e. without delay). This is a wonderful promise which is affirmed by faith. "Amen. Even so, come, Lord Jesus."

In each generation, there is a sense that Jesus is coming soon. Christians consistently talk about being in "the last days", as indeed we are. "Little children, it is the last time: and as ye have heard that antichrist shall come, even now are there many antichrists; whereby we know that it is the last time" (1 John 2:18). The soonest Jesus will come for any particular individual is when they die, and few Christians live more than one hundred years. Peter made the point that even a thousand years is not very long compared to eternity. "But, beloved, be not ignorant of this one thing, that one day is with the Lord as a thousand years, and a thousand years as one day" (2 Pet. 3:8).

While the Church waits with patience for the Second Advent, the Church waits with great hope, a sense of expectancy, a prayer of urgency. "Come, Lord Jesus." That is the hope of the Church for Jesus is the Desire of the Ages.

21 The grace of our Lord Jesus Christ *be* with you all. Amen.

The Revelation began with Jesus (Rev. 1:1), and ends with Jesus. The whole book is about Jesus, even though the name Jesus is only used fourteen times in the narrative (Rev. 1:1, 2, 9, 5; 12:17; 14:12; 17:6; 19:10; 20:4; 22:16, 20). There are many symbols in Revelation, but ultimately, each symbol has something to say about the Savior.

In his great work, *Messiah,* George Frideric Handel does not use the name of Jesus even once. Yet, the whole masterpiece, with scriptural text, is all about Jesus. Composed in 1741, the oratorio was first performed in Dublin, Ireland on April 13, 1742.

In his great work, the Revelation of Jesus Christ, the apostle John uses the name of Jesus, but mostly speaks of Him in prosaic ways, for his message is all about Christ. Jesus is the Faithful Witness. Jesus is the First Begotten of the dead. Jesus is the Prince of the kings of the earth. Jesus is the Alpha and Omega. Jesus is He that liveth and was dead. Jesus is the One who holds the seven stars in His hand. Jesus is the One who walks among the seven golden candlesticks. Jesus is the Son of God. Jesus is the One that searches the emotions and hearts. Jesus is the Lamb that was slain. Jesus is the Lion of the tribe of Juda, the Root of David. Jesus is the One who is able to unseal the scroll on which is written the decree of history. Jesus is the One who is King of kings. Jesus is the Bright and Morning Star. In every chapter, Jesus Christ is made manifest.

In His manifestation, Jesus gives grace, or unmerited favor to the undeserving. It is the grace of our Lord Jesus Christ that John wants us to have, because it is divine grace which is needed. "Lord, bless your people with grace."

> Marvelous grace of our loving Lord,
> Grace that exceeds our sin and our guilt!
> Yonder on Calvary's mount outpoured,
> There where the blood of the Lamb was spilled.
>
> Grace, grace, God's grace,
> Grace that will pardon and cleanse within;
> Grace, grace, God's grace,
> Grace that is greater than all our sin.
>
> Sin and despair, like the sea waves cold,
> Threaten the soul with infinite loss;
> Grace that is greater, yes, grace untold,
> Points to the refuge, the mighty cross.
>
> Dark is the stain that we cannot hide.
> What can avail to wash it away?
> Look! There is flowing a crimson tide,
> Brighter than snow you may be today.
>
> Marvelous, infinite, matchless grace,
> Freely bestowed on all who believe!

You that are longing to see His face,
    Will you this moment His grace receive?[2]

[2] Julie H. Johnston.

Made in the USA
Middletown, DE
08 January 2022

58221610R00136